A Fresh Look at God

Charles P. Cabell Jr.

IMPAVIDE
Publications

Copyright © 2008, 2015 Charles P. Cabell Jr.
Cover Art by David Beightol

Published by Jmars Ink

All rights reserved. No part of this book may be reproduced by any means or in any form whatsoever without written permission from the publisher, except for brief quotations embodied in literary articles or reviews.

Originally Published as:
Our Father...A Fresh Look at God by Charles P. Cabell Jr. (1997)

Impavide Publications
Colorado Springs, CO

Dedication

For my family: may they understand.

For my wife: whose idea of my retirement was more time for her.

Acknowledgements

Many people have encouraged me in this enterprise—not that they have necessarily agreed with me; emphatically some have not—but I have gained immeasurably from each in many ways: a new idea, a sharpened argument, the pointing out of an omission, a faulty or unsupported explanation, an excellent question… I am especially grateful to those who accepted my onslaught against their cherished beliefs with grace and forbearance.

A special thanks to David Beightol, for his beautiful cover.

Beightol Photo Media
Colorado Springs, CO
www.beightol.com
719-330-7327

Contents

Dedication

Acknowledgements

Foreword (to the 2nd Edition)

Preface

I: Introduction 1

II: Did *Anyone* Make Us? 12

III: God as Our Parent 18

IV: Our Parent as the "Good Parent" 28

V: What Our Parent Wants From Us...................... 36

VI: Some Limitations of Our Parent 50

VII: Sin as Obstacle to Development...................... 67

VIII: Afterlife: Reward & Punishment................... 77

IX: How to Read the Bible 89

X: Summing Up... 107

XI: Addendum: "What Then Must We Do?" 115

Bibliography 123

About the Author.. 126

Foreword (to the 2nd Edition)

I finished the First Edition in 1997. So, what made me take up the pen again and write a Second Edition? Many of my earlier readers, learning of my impending revision, asked if I had changed my mind. Actually, not at all. And I am more convinced than ever both of the general "rightness" of my earlier approach and of the continuing need to keep challenging our assumptions about God and our relationship with God.

But I might have been content to leave things where they lay except for some events and a realization. The events had to do with the trends of the last eleven years—increasing agitation for more separation between church and state, the rise of militant Islam (leading to the attacks of 9/11 and the wars in Afghanistan and Iraq), a sharpening debate between advocates of evolution and intelligent design—that have made the subject quite current.

And then there was the phenomenal success of the book, *The DaVinci Code*, which posed many of the questions I had posed six years earlier and used some the same sources I had in answering them. As a weblog put it, "Truth: Is Jesus God? Is the Bible true? Was Jesus married? Lost Books of the Bible—Are They Real? What is the Holy Grail?" Drat! If only I had been clever enough to turn my book into a novel...

So, the Second Edition was partially event-driven. But it was also realization-driven. In fact, it was mainly driven by the realization that I had left out something very important in that earlier edition, something which I have tried to correct in a new last addendum. But as T. S. Eliot implored in *The Love Song of J. Alfred Prufrock*, "Oh, do not ask, 'What is it?' Let us go and make or visit."

And in making your visit to the Second Edition, I hope that you will at least pay some attention to its structure, which is (most of the time):

1. Question
2. Elaboration/Discussion
3. Resolution
4. If (...that is true)/Then (...so what)
5. The next logical question

Each new thought stands or falls on the building blocks of thought that precede it. So I hope you will read the book from beginning to end (it is rather short, after all) and resist the temptation to go to a chapter heading or random page that intrigues and/or infuriates you and deal with the concepts found there in piecemeal fashion. If you approach it linearly, you may either agree with it or be able to see exactly where it might have gone wrong and be somewhat confident of your conclusions. Otherwise...?

Charles P. Cabell Jr.
Colorado Springs, CO
June, 2008

Preface

This is the story of my own search for faith in a God I could truly believe in and relate to. It acknowledges my crisis of faith, a crisis brought about because I was no longer able to accept traditional teachings about the nature of God and my relationship with God. The book then discusses how I resolved the crisis with a new faith based upon what I now believe is the true nature of God and our true mutual relationship.

The book is organized and presented in somewhat of an academic fashion, because I felt that if I were going to argue against orthodox views of God, my own views should be presented logically and rigorously. But the book is not an academic exercise—the subject matter is deeply felt. The structure is just to keep me (and the reader) on track.

I did not know that this would turn out to be a book. But the more I thought about things and talked to my friends, the more I realized that I could no longer hold all my thoughts in my head, particularly since I was coming to some exciting and fulfilling conclusions that I was having a hard time keeping to myself. Even so, I imagined writing only a short paper showing my thought process.

I was not afraid of writing a long paper or even a book—I had completed a 200-page dissertation as part of my doctoral program in Public Administration—but would I have enough to say, and would anyone else want to read it? After all, I had never written a book before, and I was not, shall we say, an acknowledged authority in the field of Theology. But those are the notorious "killer" thoughts that could have stopped every other budding author, so I decided to go ahead with it. I'm glad I did, whatever happens.

I truly hope that the "real" Theologians will be able to read this with an open mind, and to debate with me on the merits of the ideas rather than retreating into unassailable fortresses of "authority." My book is written from the heart with love, not written just to challenge orthodoxy. After all, we are all just trying to understand.

I: Introduction

Where did we come from? Why are we here? These questions have intrigued, puzzled, frightened, frustrated and absorbed mankind since our earliest days on the planet.

As a Catholic from birth and a product of Catholic education through eight grades of grammar school (do they still call it that?), four years of high school and my first year of college (Georgetown University), the questions and answers were readily available to me. They were confidently and unfudgingly written on the first page of the Baltimore Catechism. All Catholics had to memorize them, word for word:

"Who made us?"
"God made us."
"Who is God?"
"God is the Supreme Being."
"Why did God make us?"
"To know, love, and serve Him in this world and to be happy with Him forever in the next."

Ah, but who is God really? How could we know, love and serve Him? The answers, for Catholics, were very clear: the Church would tell us. The sources of knowledge were the Bible and tradition; but the Church would have to tell us how to interpret them. As I was growing up, I was satisfied with all of this. My mother and her family were devout Catholics and missed Mass only under dire circumstances. My father, Baptist-raised, did not go to church except with my mother and us children, and only at Christmas and Easter. But he took us to church faithfully every Sunday, and sat out in the car reading the Sunday newspaper until Mass was over. He also sent me and my brother and sister to Catholic schools, a bit of a sacrifice on a military salary. I had a few non-Catholic friends, but, at least through high school, we discussed religion very little. I became an altar boy and served daily Mass. Surrounded by Catholicism, I had no stimulus to doubt.

I spent a year at Georgetown University, a bastion of Jesuit education, but this was really a year of "prep school" for the U.S. Military Academy. Having talked my way into the first grade at age five, I was too young to enter West Point when I graduated from high school at sixteen. Georgetown was willing to give me a half scholarship, so I took it.

As I am writing this Second Edition, there is a huge controversy swirling about concerning the role of religion in U.S. national affairs. The Supreme Court has just laid down rather confusing guidelines about display of the Ten Commandments in and around public buildings. The service academies (particularly the Air Force Academy) are wrestling with whether statements by Commandants and emails by cadet/midshipman leaders denote undue favoritism toward Christianity in violation of the Constitution.

But at the West Point of my day (1954-1958), little of these kinds of religious "sensitivity" issues bubbled to the surface. The majority of cadets were Protestants, followed by Catholics and Jews. I am not aware of any Muslims in the class, but we did have a couple of cadets from Thailand who were Buddhists.

Whatever you were, you were required to go to *some* church service over the weekend. The Protestants went to the magnificent Cadet Chapel, a beautiful military-gothic structure overlooking the entire Academy that had the second largest pipe organ in the Western Hemisphere (I never learned where the *first* largest was). The Catholics went to the Catholic Chapel, a more modest but equally handsome structure a short walk away. Jewish cadets had their own chapel, much more modest yet and a longer walk from the cadet area. Even the avowed atheists (and Buddhists) had to sign up for one service or another. Generally they picked a religious service that was: a) least offensive to their belief system proclivities; or (more likely) b) most congenial as to time and distance.

So the prevailing atmosphere at West Point was a generic encouragement of religion. Belief in *something* was good. We even had our own Cadet Prayer, written by the Reverend Clayton E. Wheat, USMA Chaplain 1918-1926, and later English Department Chairman 1926-1945.

I: Introduction

The West Point Cadet Prayer

O God, our Father, thou Searcher of men's hearts, help us to draw near to thee in sincerity and truth.

May our religion be filled with gladness and may our worship of thee be natural.

Strengthen and increase our admiration for honest dealing and clean thinking, and suffer not our hatred of hypocrisy and pretense ever to diminish.

Encourage us in our endeavor to live above the common level of life.

Make us to choose the harder right instead of the easier wrong, and never to be content with a half-truth when the whole can be won.

Endow us with courage that is born of loyalty to all that is noble and worthy, that scorns to compromise with vice and injustice and knows no fear when truth and right are in jeopardy.

Guard us against flippancy and irreverence in the sacred things of life.

Grant us new ties of friendship and new opportunities of service.

Kindle our hearts in fellowship with those of a cheerful countenance, and soften our hearts with sympathy for those who sorrow and suffer.

Help us to maintain the honor of the Corps untarnished and unsullied and to show forth in our lives the ideals of West Point in doing our duty to thee and to our Country.

All of which we ask in the name of the Great Friend and Master of Men.

A wonderful prayer; it captures the ideals of West Point very nicely. And it is generic enough that it would not have been offensive to anyone except those whose religious views were very narrow. There is no mention of Jesus Christ, and the "Great Friend and Master of men" could even have been Buddha. I read this prayer at the funeral of my father, USMA 1925.

But despite the tolerant tenor of the place, Catholics like me were clearly in the minority. For the first time in my life, I found myself in serious religious discussions with intelligent—and sometimes belligerent—non-Catholics, often well after "Taps," while risking the righteous wrath of the Officer-in-Charge, who prowled the hallways looking for restless cadets. But I was not open-minded and quickly became angered at challenges to my cherished beliefs.

I stayed very active in the Church, often going to daily Mass before breakfast. Actually, this was freighted with extra advantage during my Plebe (first) year. If you went to Mass, you could go to breakfast late straight from Mass, thus avoiding the normal hazing that went on during breakfast formation. You would also avoid a particularly heinous form of special hazing known as "Calls," in which some zealous or aggrieved upperclassman ordered you to his room between reveille and breakfast and had you—while you stood in an exaggerated "brace"—spout the "Plebe Poop" you were supposed to have memorized, and/or made you perform some distasteful physical exercise (like a zillion push-ups) until time to form up before breakfast. The announcement that you wished to go to Mass made said upperclassman hesitate to buck the Almighty and a reprieve or outright excusal generally ensued.

As an aside, after I had employed the Mass tactic probably a few times too often, one frustrated upperclassman wondered out loud if I would still display the same devotion in my upper-class years when I was no longer subject to "Calls." I resented his implication at the time, but I have to admit that I did not go to Mass nearly as often in my last three years at the Point. But my faith never wavered. I also sang in the Catholic Choir, and was co-director of the Choir during my senior year. I graduated from West Point in 1958.

After West Point, I continued my strong affiliation with the Catholic Church, and was a choir member or choir director during several of my ensuing military assignments. I went on to a thirty-year career in the Air Force, retiring as a Brigadier General.

At some point, however—and it was gradual, not sudden, so it's hard to pin down a date—I had begun to examine my spiritual life more critically. I found that I had been going through the motions for some time. And if I were honest with myself, that time was a long time indeed. I still attended Mass regularly (on Sunday, not daily as in my Plebe year at West Point), but I began to realize that my attendance at Mass was no longer, if, in fact, it ever had been, motivated by a deep love for the Creator. I went because of fear or habit. My attention at Mass wandered all over the place, and seldom focused on the Almighty. My prayers at Mass and at home were ritualistic, not heartfelt. I felt confused by what I was reading in the Bible, and unsatisfied by official explanations coming from the Church.

My wife was non-Catholic (Episcopalian), and in order for us to get married in the Catholic Church, she had to agree that our children would be raised as Catholics. The real problem was me. In raising our two children (we adopted a girl and a boy, two years apart), I dutifully sent them to Sunday school, but as they grew up, I was always reluctant to preach Catholicism to them. When they began to drift away from the Church, I made little to no effort to shepherd them back. My faith at that point was barely sufficient to keep me going; I had none left for them.

The main problem for me was the way God was being portrayed: back to the question of "Who is God really?" Stick your finger in the Old Testament anywhere at random and it will likely land on a passage of wrath, vengeance, death and destruction. As depicted in the Old Testament, and to a lesser extent in the New Testament, God is someone to be feared, not loved. Would God really condemn the descendants of Adam and Eve because of their transgression (Genesis 3)? Would God really slaughter innocents whose gate had not been marked with the blood of a lamb just so that Moses would be allowed to lead the children of Israel out of Egypt (Exodus 12)? Would God really destroy Israeli cities because of the sin of David in ordering a census against God's will (Samuel 24)? Even in the New Testament account, would God really give Peter the ability to curse to death Ananias and his wife, Sapphira, for the terrible sin of generously selling their own land to give to the apostles, but keeping a part of the price for themselves (Acts 5)?

The internet has yielded other examples—some amusing, but still thought-provoking—since I wrote the First Edition. Leviticus 25:44 suggests that owning slaves is acceptable as long as they are from neighboring regions (one wag wondered if that meant that it was OK to make slaves out of Canadians and Mexicans). Deuteronomy 23:1 says that "he who is wounded in the stones [testicles] or hath his privy member cut off shall not enter into the congregation of the Lord." Tough luck, John Wayne Bobbitt (you may recall what his wife, Lorena, deprived him of as he slept). Worse yet, "a bastard shall not enter into the congregation of the Lord; even to the tenth generation ..." Deuteronomy 23:2. Clearly, the (poor) bastard had no role in the initial sin that resulted in his/her birth, yet ten generations must suffer for his/her non-crime? Does any of this make any sense at all? Is God really like that?

I am not the first to ask these questions. The general line of the answers, however, has been to accept the Bible accounts as true, and then either to weave a convoluted response that tries to reconcile all these difficulties, or—the unassailable response—to shrug a holy shrug and say that only God can answer them (and, by the way, who am I to question God?).

Another line of answers offers the concept that the reason God is depicted so differently in the Old and New Testaments is that God has, in fact, changed: that He has learned how to deal with men better and is taking a new tack. I think that a better explanation is that it is not God who has changed, but man's understanding of Him, and that the New Testament reflects that better understanding. But would anyone say that we understand Him well enough yet?

In my weakening and now questioned faith, I was dangerously close to making one of two choices. I could shrug and just keep going through the motions; or (and I believed, worse), I could drift away into agnosticism and ignore my spiritual side entirely. But then there was a breakthrough that suggested that I could reason my way back into a faith that I could embrace wholeheartedly. Yes, I said, "reason my way to faith." Although this seems paradoxical, that is what this book is about.

The breakthrough for me came when I was reading a very sad book. A neighbor brought it to me when she saw mention of my father's name in it. The book is *An American Requiem* by James Carroll. In it, Carroll, the son of an Air Force General, tells the story of how he became a priest during the Vietnam War, and found himself at odds with his father and the Catholic Church. My father was mentioned because, as an Air Force General himself, he and the Carrolls were neighbors at Bolling AFB.

I: Introduction

What struck me in the book was a very short passage in which Carroll described the relationship between Christ and God. In the New Testament, Christ did not address God as "Oh Mighty Potentate," "Oh August Personage," or the like, but "Abba:" Father. Or, as Carroll explains it, "Daddy."

I cannot tell you how much that passage moved me. Suddenly, many things became clear. I decided to rethink the whole notion of a relationship between God and man in terms of "Daddy-Child," rather than in the rather arms-length relationship of "God-Subject." This book is the result.

I take on this task with great humility and the realization that I could be terribly wrong. I am not a trained theologian. Over the last several years I have read a number of books which bore upon the subject of alternate views of God, but I stopped consulting outside sources after the "Daddy" insight. For one reason, I looked upon my book as an exercise in pure thought. I did not want to be overly swayed by the ideas of others until I had a chance to clarify my own. Or maybe it was because I was afraid I would learn that someone else had thought it through better.

I had shared some of my thoughts with friends (at least those I did not think would judge me crazy or arrogant for taking on such a project) and had learned that—far from dispelling my doubt—they were struggling with many of the same things I was.

So I put together this treatise without doing a whole lot of research (but some, as you will see) and without a lot of personal consultation. On the whole, the thoughts herein are mine alone.

I do not wish to offend anyone, but undoubtedly the ideas contained herein will cause some discomfort if not outright rage. My hope, however, is that it will encourage others to develop and experience the kind of "Daddy-Child" relationship I have described. Is God really "Daddy?" Who can be sure (although one of the nice things about the topic is that no one can prove me absolutely wrong)? But wouldn't it be wonderful if it were so?

II: Did *Anyone* Make Us?

For many people, the hardest concept to get past is whether we were *created* or whether we simply *evolved*. Are we the result of an intelligent, directive force, or did we just crawl out of the primordial ooze all by ourselves after millions of years of faulty starts? Before we can even discuss the "Daddy-Child" relationship, we must establish the existence of "Daddy."

To me, there is no inherent conflict between creationism and evolution except for the starting point. It is pretty clear that some sort of evolution has been going on for eons. But organisms do not evolve from nothingness: evolution needs ingredients, some combination of matter and energy to build upon. Where did all this matter and energy come from? Were they always just "there," or did someone who has always existed decide to put them there?

I have no problem with the concept that if there exists a Being powerful and intelligent enough to create us as we exist today, that Being could have chosen to do so either by a single mighty "Shazam!!" or by setting up the process of evolution.

The answer to the question whether we were

created or whether the components of our DNA evolved from pre-existing matter and energy cannot be derived objectively and scientifically. In the absence of some unmistakable sign from heaven, the answer must be inferential.

There are several classic "proofs" (I will call them "indications") of God's existence. Probably the most famous is Aristotle's principle of causality. Which came first, the chicken or the egg? Well, eggs come from chickens; chickens come from eggs. But at some point, Aristotle argued, there must have been a first chicken or a first egg. That is, there must have been a "Prime Mover" for chickens, eggs, and everything else in the universe. Thomas Aquinas and Descartes used this argument also.

Another indication is that every human being seems to be born with a conscience, a sense of right and wrong. On the whole, virtue is admired, and man tries to be good, using the "Golden Rule" (i.e., "Do unto others as you would have them do unto you.") as a moral compass. Now, one could argue that the "Golden Rule" has nothing to do with morality or conscience, and everything to do with some biological mandate to preserve the species. Clearly, failure to abide by the Rule beyond certain limits would result in the self-destruction of society. Still, there is no denying the lift that people get from being good and performing good works, and the anguish they suffer from causing pain (with many exceptions, of course). It is difficult to conceive that conscience really could have come from matter and energy alone.

Another indication is that there is more to life than mere survival. In 1954, Abraham Maslow, a psychologist interested in organizational psychology, identified a "Hierarchy of Psychological Needs" that has been debated by management theorists ever since. His five-level need hierarchy from *Motivation and Personality* (as reported by Harmon and Mayer in *Organization Theory for Public Administration*, 1986) is as follows:

1. *Physiological.* Chiefly food and shelter.
2. *Safety.* Freedom from physical harm and deprivation.
3. *Love.* The desire for affectionate and supportive relationships with family, friends and associates.
4. *Esteem.* The recognition by others of one's competence, achievements, and overall personal worth.
5. *Self-Actualization (or self-realization).* The need to realize one's inherent potential, one's creative abilities, "to be everything one is capable of becoming."

These beyond-survival aspects of our existence, which go well beyond the arrangement of molecules in our individual DNA, are hard to explain without our connection to a higher power.

The last indication I will document is captured very well in a long quote from Sigmund Freud's book,

Civilization and its Discontents (1930). Freud, having sent his friend, Romain Rolland, a book he had written treating religion as an illusion, received the reply that Freud paraphrases below:

> The true source of religious sentiments consists in a peculiar feeling, which he himself is never without, which he finds confirmed by many others, and which he may suppose is present in millions of people. It is a feeling which he would like to call a sensation of 'eternity,' a feeling as of something limitless, unbounded—as it were, 'oceanic.' This feeling, he adds, is a purely subjective fact, not an article of faith; it brings with it no assurance of personal immortality, but it is the source of the religious energy which is seized upon by the various Churches and religious systems, directed by them into particular channels, and doubtless also exhausted by them. One may, he thinks, rightly call oneself religious on the ground of this oceanic feeling alone, even if one rejects every belief and every illusion.

I share that "oceanic" feeling (Freud regretted that he did not). This almost universal yearning for something "limitless," "unbounded," is a clear indication of the existence of a limitless, unbounded Being that humans need to connect with.

Taken one at a time, these "indications" are hardly "proofs" at all. Simply because we yearn for something eternal does not mean that something or someone eternal exists. Aristotle's "First Cause" could be simply the matter and energy that has existed for all time in other forms than chickens and eggs.

But taken as a whole, these indications are hard to ignore and refute. As a "yearning" human being myself, I want there to be a God, and this bias undoubtedly affects my judgment. I also worry, along with Romain Rolland, that the various churches and religious systems have tapped into these yearning-born biases in ways that have confused us and kept us away from, not close to, the "real" God. I believe in God, but no longer the God I grew up with.

Nowhere in these indications is the answer to the question of whether God is a unitary being or a distributed being. Those of us who have been brought up in the Judeo-Christian tradition tend to think of God as a unitary being, helped along in that belief by artists who have painted God, as a friend of mine put it, as "a white guy with a beard sitting on a throne."

The Hindu tradition is quite different. As Will Durant explained in *Our Oriental Heritage* (1935), taking from the *Upanishads*, the essence of God is found in the ideas of *Atman* and *Brahman*:

> *Atman*, the Self of all selves, the Soul of all souls, the immaterial, formless Absolute in which we bathe ourselves when we forget ourselves... *Brahman*, the one pervading, neuter, impersonal, all-embracing, underlying, tangible essence of the world, the 'Real of the Real,' the 'unborn Soul, undecaying, undying' the Soul of all Things as *Atman* is the Soul of all Souls; the one force that stands behind, beneath and above all forces

and all gods.

The Hindu tradition seems closer to the idea of God as the presence detected by Freud's friend, Romain Rolland: that "oceanic" feeling.

Operationally, it makes no difference whether God is unitary, distributed, or some combination of the two—or none of the above—as long as we can establish good two-way communications. In the next chapters, I will write of God (and communications with God) under the assumption that God is a unitary being because it is less clumsy that way; but I am open to the other possibilities.

Having convinced myself of the existence of God, it was time to undertake a deeper exploration of God's nature.

III: God as Our Parent

Why do we call God "Our Father?" Why such a masculine term? In polytheistic religions, there is room for deities of both sexes. In the monotheistic Judeo-Christian tradition, there is room for only one. Since there was no word in the ancient (or modern) languages for a combination male/female, the ancients had to make a choice. The Greek word *hermaphrodite* seems to capture the idea of a being with dual sexual organs but not a being with all of the emotional and personality characteristics we associate with males and females.

One explanation for why the ancients chose to think of God as male has to do with authority. The tendency in olden times was to attribute to a god or gods whatever the people could not understand. Violent acts of nature, such as floods and pestilence, or even violent acts of man, such as wars of conquest, were thought to be the result of Divine anger. In the patriarchal society of the times, the authority figures were overwhelmingly masculine. It would seem natural to consider the ultimate authority figure, one who could command nature and man, as masculine also.

This was by no means universal, however. According to Karen Armstrong in her remarkable book, *The History of God* (1993), during the Paleolithic period, when agriculture was emerging, the cult of the Mother Goddess attracted groups from Europe, the Near East, and all the way to India. These fertility cults remained important for centuries. Eventually, however, the man-centered, man-managed religions became ascendant and pushed the others aside.

But is our God really only male? Nearly every biological species has both a masculine and feminine form, and it takes the two together to produce new life. Why should not the same be true of God? In fact, in the early Jewish mythology, Yahweh had a female consort. Of course if God is a true spirit, the notion of dual sexuality is meaningless, but perhaps not the notion of the single Divinity having both male and female characteristics.

The question may arise: "Whose male and female characteristics," because in some biological species we can observe characteristics in males and females that do not correspond well to those found in humans. In some cases, the traditional roles seem to be reversed. Males are not the dominant gender in bonobo society, for example. The bonobo is similar to the chimpanzee, but was recognized as an entirely separate species in 1928.

Some more disagreement may be found from new and old sources in areas as disparate as psychological treatises and Asian medicine. One modern view may be found in John Gray's book, *Men are from Mars, Women are from Venus* (1992). A more ancient view may be found in the Asian concept of the feminine *yin* (meaning dark, or shade) qualities and the masculine *yang* (meaning bright, or light) qualities, extending at least as far back as the 8th century BC.

Somewhere between the modern and the ancient views is what I am talking about. But is that really important? The important things would seem to be that the characteristics are differentiable and that both are necessary.

Roman Catholic theology posits a *triune* God—one God, but three persons in the one God: Father, Son and Holy Spirit. But this conclusion was not easily come by. In fact, disagreements about this almost ripped apart the early Church. In order to preserve Church unity, the Emperor Constantine called for the first ecumenical (universal) council of the Church to be held in the hall of an imperial palace in the town of Nicaea near his capital, Nicomedia, in 325AD. The main purpose of the Council was to resolve the controversy, which had been festering for almost three-hundred years, over whether Christ was a created being "similar" (in Greek, *homoiousia*) to God the Father or an eternal being "consubstantial" (*homoousia*) with the Father.

As Will Durant described in *Caesar and Christ* (1944), 318 bishops from all over the empire showed up. Not too surprising since Constantine was generous enough to pay their way and all expenses, although most of the visitors were from the eastern (closer) provinces. Pope Sylvester I, detained by illness, sent a few priests. Many more priests and lower-order churchmen attended the bishops.

The main proponent for the created Christ was Bishop Arius, who had gathered many supporters in his native city of Alexandria, Egypt. Arius also believed that the Holy Spirit was a lesser God begotten by Christ. His opponent was the brilliant and pugnacious Bishop Athanasius, who beat down the naive and less-eloquent Arius in debate.

Constantine was present at many of the sessions and participated in the debates. His was not a theological interest: he preferred the view that Christ was God because the unity and authority of the Church was built on that premise. Without it, the Church, and therefore the State, might crumble.

Together, the Bishops put together what is now the Nicene Creed. It was not something handed down on stone tablets from a nearby mountain; it was a compromise document with theological and political undertones. Votes were taken, and the supporters of wording that would have suggested a *created*, not divine, Christ went from seventeen, to five, to two: Arius and one other.

From the beginning, the supporters of Arius said that they would sign the document if they were allowed to change the document by "one *iota*," i.e. the Greek letter, I. Since that one iota, changing *homoousia* to *homoiousia* made all the difference, the other bishops refused to support the change. Arius was anathematized by the Council and exiled by the

III: God as Our Parent

Emperor. All of Arius's books were ordered to be burned and anyone caught concealing one would be punished by death.

Christ was pronounced *divine*.

Ockham's Razor, the idea that the simplest explanation is usually correct, would support a simpler theory, and it is the one I suggest here. It makes more sense to me that in reality we have a *diune* God—one God, but *two* persons, not three, in the one God. For lack of better terms, perhaps these are the persons we have been calling the "Father" and the "Holy Spirit." The Father may be said to represent male characteristics (whatever they are); the Holy Spirit may be said to represent female characteristics (whatever they are).

The point is that God is not masculine alone. The human race is more logically the product of some sort of divine intercourse (figuratively speaking, of course: I do not want to sound too anthropomorphic here) between the two persons. The Creator mirrors the created. God is both Father and Mother. We are all His/Her children.

At this juncture, a dear friend of mine in England, reacting to an earlier draft of my book, raised a question triggered by the current speculation about the possibility of other intelligent species in the universe. Other species might not even have parents as such. What if an entire species was created all at the same time, for example (as some people believe angels came to be)? He questioned whether the God-as-parent concept would even be applicable to other species. He reasoned that God would have to be God for the whole universe (I agree), and that the God I was describing was too narrow and limited. Interesting point! My only answer is that a universal God could interact with other species in different ways but still act as a parent with us.

Also at this point, reviewing the same earlier draft of this treatise, my daughter, then lawyer-to-be, challenged the consistency of my logic. I suggested that the decision to include the notion of a *triune* God as a matter of faith to be documented in the Nicene Creed may have been arrived at in a somewhat arbitrary manner, contaminated, perhaps, by political considerations within and without the Church. Okay. But then my own conclusion, that God was a diune God, seemed to her just as arbitrary. (Actually, it probably seemed to her *more* arbitrary, but she was being somewhat sparing in her criticism because I am her father. I like that in a daughter!) I have no ready answer for that, except that for me the notion of a diune God is more satisfying and less awkward, and seems to mirror nature better.

To be consistent with this diune construction, however, I have had to downgrade in my own mind the status of what had been the second person of the Holy Trinity: the Son, Jesus Christ. I know that other religions, including some "Christian" ones—Constantine or no Constantine—have never held to the divinity of Christ. But this was very difficult for me, a Catholic, and I did not reach this position lightly. Other things persuaded me besides just

III: God as Our Parent

Ockham's Razor, and I will discuss them later.

Thus, the first important tenet of this fresh view of God is that God is now to be considered "Daddy/<u>Mommy</u>." To capture the notion of a diune God who has created us as His/Her children, I will refer to this "new" God as "Our Parent."

I will, however, continue to use the term "God" to preserve historical context (the Being described in *Genesis* will continue to be called "God") and to honor the name that has been passed down to us for many generations. When I want to highlight the difference between the traditional, historical God and the new God I am trying to describe, I will use the term "Our Parent." I hope this is not too confusing.

But what is Our Parent like? I could take refuge in the scholarly treatises of the past for the answer, but that would undoubtedly lead me down the same paths that eventually left me unsatisfied. Instead, I consider that Our Parent could be—in the simplest possible terms—good, bad, whimsical, or a combination of the three.

I reason that Our Parent *has* to be *good* or He/She would be impossible for mankind to deal with. How could we hope to satisfy a bad, whimsical, or variable Parent? The same human act could sometimes please and sometimes displease. We would be forever waiting for a cosmic "Gotcha," and we wouldn't know why.

I remember a Monty Python TV episode in which an interviewee (Eric Idle, perhaps) was trying to land a job with a whimsical interviewer played by John

Cleese. Eric was killing himself trying to please and impress John Cleese, but the feedback he was getting from Cleese was inconsistent, if not totally baffling. Eric would make some point or other and Cleese would nod enthusiastic approval. Thinking he'd finally gotten the idea, Idle would follow up with another point along the same lines. This time, Cleese would frown and shake his head. Poor Eric Idle was a basket case after only a few minutes of this.

And so are we when we are totally baffled by or perceive a lack of consistency in the one thought to be our Creator and Master. When some disaster befalls us, we conclude that the god(s) must be angry, and we cast about for a few terrified virgins to sacrifice to them. When by chance it seems to work, it is not healthy to be a virgin for a while. But then it doesn't work, and we try something equally bizarre. No, if we humans have any chance at all, then Our Parent must be not only good, but predictably and consistently good.

The whole rest of the book is based upon the premise that God is Our Parent and, unlike some human parents, is totally and consistently good. The alternative is just too horrible to contemplate.

This premise means that all religious writings—past and present—about God would have to be judged against the standard: "Gee, would a good Parent really act that way?" To return to an earlier example: "Would a good Parent really condemn the innocent descendants of Adam and Eve to a lifetime of misery and pain because of the single transgression of their earthly parents?" I do not believe so.

How about this? Taken further, "Would a good Parent really condemn His/Her own Son to unimaginable suffering on the Cross just to appease Him/Her for the sin of Adam and Eve?" I have a hard time with that one too.

You can see where I am going. Against that simple but very powerful standard, much of the Old and New Testaments is reduced to allegory, myth, or the mistaken attempts of earnest people thousands of years ago to explain their universe. More on this later, in Chapter IX: How to Read the Bible.

I can be rightly challenged on the basis that I am trying to apply human reason against Divine purposes, which may be like trying to use a wooden ruler to measure magnetism: wholly inappropriate and wrong-headed. But I am only trying to do what countless other humans have tried to do. Moreover, I am attempting to do so in such a manner that the construction is at least internally consistent, which I do not believe the current orthodox ones are.

Another alternative to attempting to understand the Divine through reason, of course, is to abandon reason altogether and say something like: "Lord, I acknowledge Your unfathomableness. I understand nothing, but that matters not at all. All I need to know is how to increase the love that binds us together." I have known people who seem to connect with God in just such a way, and I have found myself envious of their serenity. Perhaps I will get there myself someday, worn out with the futility of reasoning. But

I am nowhere near there yet.

Maybe my brain gets in the way too much. All I know now is that my brain *is* in the way because of the inconsistencies I see in the ways God is currently viewed and my unwillingness to chalk up the differences to "the mysterious ways of Divine Providence."

Besides, God gave us a brain. My brain tells me that much of what we attribute to "the mysterious ways of Divine Providence" could be explained by changing our ideas of who God is and what He/She is. Thus I am emboldened to continue.

My ultimate motivation in doing all this is to understand Our Parent better, so that through that understanding I can improve, if possible, my own relationship with Him/Her, helping to lead me to a more fulfilled life.

The next question, then, is "What is a good parent?"

IV: Our Parent as the "Good Parent"

Why did God want to become Our Parent in the first place? Why would He/She want to have children? The one-liner Baltimore Catechism answer was: to "know, love and serve God in this world and to be happy with Him in the next." But let's explore this in the context of God as the "Good Parent."

Let's use ourselves as an analogy. If *we* are "good parents," why do *we* have children? I believe that when we *choose* to have children (as opposed to when they just happen) we are motivated by love and a sense that our lives will be more fulfilled by having children. Having had them, we tend to regret having to discipline them; we would much prefer to be able to lavish our affection on them without fear of spoiling them. Aren't we happier when we can do something for our children than when they can do something for us? Our Parent *chose* to have children. Might not His/Her motivations have been the same as ours? Might not His/Her nurturing attitudes be the same? Would not Our Parent want more for and from His/Her children than lifelong servitude? And God is not just the "Good Parent;" God would have to be the "Perfect Parent."

How would we define the perfect parent? Ironically, it was James Carroll's painful relationship with his own (in his view, imperfect) parents that gave me the insight I needed to write this book. My own parents were wonderful and I loved them dearly. I suppose they were not perfect, but I would find it hard to fault them in any singular respect. I would certainly rate them as better parents than I am. My son got married since the First Edition was written, and he and his wife have given us five wonderful grandsons. Even he and his wife are better parents to their children than I was to him. It ain't easy.

In fact, the biggest trouble a dear, dear friend of mine had with this book was trying to relate to my notion of the "Good Parent." I knew her parents (or thought I did), but the psychological warfare that went on around her house left her with deep scars that she carries to this day. She could never really grasp what I was talking about. Very sad. So, here we are again. What does it mean to be a "Good Parent?"

Parenting theories abound. They range from the old saw, "Spare the rod and spoil the child," to my dear cousin's philosophy, "Why have kids if you can't spoil them?" Now clearly the rod-user in this context is not a sadist, gaining some sort of satisfaction from his/her children's pain. "This is going to hurt me more than it hurts you" is almost literally true, although the child has difficulty believing it at the time. It is just that the parent believes in the necessity for strong, direct discipline. On the other hand, my cousin did not truly want to "spoil" her daughters, foisting two evil little brats on an undeserving society. She simply believed (to her very soul until the very end) that there is no such thing as too much love, and that unconstrained love does not automatically lead to spoiling. What can I say? She raised two daughters who are delights in every way. But these two viewpoints represent a very wide spectrum. Is there common ground?

The common ground seems to be centered along three lines: love, encouragement, and the willingness to give individual attention. If Our Parent is the Perfect Parent, then we, as His/Her children, should expect those in abundance. But we should also expect a maturing relationship with Our Parent as we ourselves mature. We should not be treated as children forever.

Let's take love first. A perfect parent would bestow unconditional love, not forcing the child to earn it. If the child acts badly, the perfect parent would deplore the act and not love any less the child who committed it. As earthly parents, faced with less-than-perfect children (particularly during the teenage years), we might have trouble following that principle at times; but the perfect parent should not.

How wonderful! That means that whatever evil we do, we can still always count on the unwavering love of Our Parent. That does not give us license to be malevolent, but it should give us hope and comfort during the times when we falter.

Next, let's take encouragement. The perfect parent encourages; he/she does not force. On the divine scale, this gets us into the area of free will.

But the Old Testament story of David (II Samuel) suggests that man's free will is at least limited. After David had stolen Bathsheba from Uriah and had sent him into the "forefront of the hottest battle" to be killed, Nathan the prophet came to see him. Because of David's sin, Nathan said, the Lord was going to "raise up evil against thee out of thine own house." In due course, Amnon, one of David's sons, raped Tamar, the sister of Absalom, another of David's sons (David had a number of wives). In grief and outrage, Absalom had Amnon killed. Next, Absalom plotted against his father, David, and was himself eventually slain, causing David even more sorrow.

As I read it, had David not sinned in the first place, things would have turned out differently. Were Amnon and Absalom exercising their free will, or was the Lord using them as agents of His punishment of David? This is a disturbing story when interpreted the second way.

If we do not have free will, we do not have choice. We would be robots, with a little battery in our backs and a little computer in our brains, programmed by the Almighty, not responsible for our actions. Without free will, life would be a cruel joke. Some people might seemingly be favored by the Almighty (like David, perhaps), others cursed, with no opportunity to grow. How would a Good Parent treat free will? Possibly more important, how does our free will interact with the notion of God's will?

Let's go back to the analogy of earthly good parents. You are a good parent. How do you let your children's choices interact with your own preferences? You do not program your children; you guide and encourage them. In fact, my parents were careful not to push me or my siblings toward any particular career or life paths. I believe that Our Parent works with us in the same way.

Thus I have come to conclude that "God's will" is a misnomer. One construct of the world is that God has a plan, and that man's job is to discover what that plan is and follow it. But, as parents ourselves, do we really have a *plan* for our children, or do we have *hopes* and *aspirations* for them? Even if we think we know what is best for them, is it not more satisfying to watch them (and help them) discover their own best paths? It is more satisfying for them and it is more satisfying for us.

Of course, when our children are young, we necessarily impose our will on them to teach them, to discipline them, and to ensure their safety. But our whole job as parents is to prepare them to be independent of us, to ease them out of the nest and let them fly alone. Our Parent has entrusted that part of the job to us. Once grown, our children form a <u>new</u> relationship with us and Our Parent as well.

In both cases, the new relationship is more that of friendship than of obeisance. Our earthly mother and father, except in situations of clear overdependence, gradually back away, leaving us to make our own decisions. They rejoice in our good fortune but are willing to help if needed. In the best of families, the love and respect for our parents remain and, indeed, strengthen; but the previous formality is replaced by an easy companionship. The one-way "thou-shalts and shalt-nots" give way to real two-way conversations of genuine intimacy. I could experience those things happening with my earthly parents, but I could not seem to experience them with God.

Why not? If God is truly the Good Parent, wouldn't He/She want it that way? And wouldn't it be much nicer for us as well? It seems to me now that the only obstacles to achieving such a maturing relationship with Our Parent are those we place there ourselves. As we grow up, we need to seek to de-emphasize the worshipful and adorational aspects of our relationship with Our Parent, because they tend to keep us at arm's length. We need to seek to develop with Our Parent the same kind of relationship we seek to develop with our earthly parents: a close, caring, loving, respecting, communicating, easy, confidence-sharing, personal familiarity, unencumbered by the fear of needing to hold back.

Your earthly parents nurtured you through the dirty-diaper stage, the terrible teens, and your sometimes unsuccessful youthful struggles to make it in the world. There are no pretenses left. Our two kids put us through the wringer for a while, but we are wonderful friends now. I am left to conclude that the struggle is part of Our Parent's plan. If our teenagers stayed cuddly and cute, we couldn't stand to let them go. This way, we don't mind so much. And when they figuratively come back, the relationship is definitely changed and everyone is the better for it.

The same is true of your friends from youth. You can achieve a very relaxed state with them *because* they know you so well. They have seen you at your worst and best, and there are few real surprises remaining. They will love you almost no matter what. I believe that this is possible and greatly desired in our relationship with Our Parent also.

Finally, let's take individual attention. The good earthly parent does not treat his/her children the same. Yes, we try to balance out the distribution of gifts and the like to maintain fairness, but we do not give exactly the same gift to each child. Not everyone gets a football for Christmas. A football for your violin-playing son (or daughter) might not be viewed as a gift at all, and might even be resented. You take care to give each of your children what you know would appeal to them (as long as it would not cause them harm). This gives satisfaction to you and also to your child.

You do not talk to all of your children in the same way. What would motivate one would be utterly lost on another. With one you would appeal to reason; with another you would appeal to emotion. What would cause one to feel punished would not bother another in the least. For example, my mother would send my extravert brother to sit on the stairs and count to a thousand when he had strayed too far from righteous behavior. To be removed from society for even a short time would darned near kill him. As an introvert, I considered quiet time alone a gift; as a bit of a rebel, I required stronger and more direct methods.

Our Parent created each of us as a unique being, with our own gifts, shortcomings, and sense of reward and punishment. As a perfect parent, Our Parent would acknowledge and make use of these in helping to guide and encourage us in our lives.

I have not yet discussed the *mechanisms* by which Our Parent shows His/Her love, provides encouragement, and gives us individual attention, but I will do so in the chapters to come. We have been discussing what we should expect from Our Parent; now let's discuss what Our Parent expects from us, His/Her children.

V: What Our Parent Wants From Us

The Baltimore Catechism answer to this question was to "know, love and serve God in this world and to be happy with Him in the next."

If you buy my arguments to this point, you might also buy that Our Parent really wants our love, as we want our children to love us.

What about the quality of that love? Our Parent could have *forced* us to love Him/Her. In the shudderingly eerie anti-utopian novel *1984*, written in 1949, George Orwell's main character learned to "love" "Big Brother" through brainwashing and torture. Our Parent could have done that, creating us as little robots, serving His/Her every whim with "love," unable, in fact, to do anything else. But where would be the satisfaction to Our Parent in that? "Love Me, little Robot!" "Sure, Oh Mighty One." Genuine satisfaction comes from being loved by someone who really knows you and chooses to love you. This gets us back to the idea of the maturing relationship also.

Which gives *you,* as parents, the most pleasure: the love shown by your children when they were small or the love shown by your children after they have grown up? Having experienced both myself, I find that I have enjoyed both but that there is something truly special about the grown-up kind when your children have had a real chance to make an informed judgment about your worthiness to be loved. I always get at least a micro-lump in my throat whenever my grown up son or daughter calls just to say hello. I believe Our Parent must feel much the same way. So, knowledge and choice would seem to be necessary ingredients for achieving "quality" love.

A friend of mine has suggested that, on the Divine scale, at least, knowledge and choice are connected. If Our Parent made His/Her power and influence too obvious (increasing our knowledge), perhaps we would feel coerced into paying attention (reducing our choices). Thus it makes sense that Our Parent would reveal Himself/Herself in limited ways only, not in some monthly heavenly extravaganza or documentable personal appearances.

With Our Parent's reluctance to make blatantly manifest His/Her interest in us, the burden falls upon *us* to seek such knowledge about Our Parent. But I believe Our Parent will share such knowledge when asked in quiet sessions of prayer.

One of the ideas that kept me close to organized religion (Roman Catholicism) was that I was hung up on the notion that God had a preference for how He wished to be worshiped. It is irrelevant how I wish to worship God; it is how God wishes that I worship Him that counts. The power and appeal of the Catholic Church is that it claims to know, and has the Mass, the Sacraments, all of the other rituals and rites, and an infallible Pope to structure a set of worships that is pleasing to Him. Gosh! The "one-right-wayness" of all this may be attractive to people with an engineering mind set, but it is awfully rigid.

In many ways, this view of God-worship is a substitute for thinking. Don't think; do as we tell you. That's what I allowed to happen to me. I had memorized all the prayers, but after a while I no longer thought about what the prayers were really saying. Perhaps it was just me, but I don't think so.

When I went to someone's (non-Catholic) house for dinner, their "grace" was a conversation with God about how nice it was to share a meal with a friend, and an invitation to God to share in it as well. My grace, along with the graces of many of my fellow Catholics, was a formulaic incantation, dutifully memorized and flawlessly repeated, but it lacked conviction and warmth.

Almost thirty-five years ago, my wife and I visited the little village of Chichicastenango, in Guatemala. The pride of the village was a beautiful church dating from the time of the Conquistadores (mid 1500's). Inside the church, there were all sorts of things that, shall we say, appeared somewhat unorthodox. There were leather shoes on the feet of the statues and cloth shawls and serapes around the shoulders of the plaster saints. A long box, about eight inches tall and several feet across, full of sand and dozens of little candles both lit and unlit, ran down the main aisle. On the steps of the church, an Indian "Witch Doctor," or "Shaman," was performing some religious rite with a number of people in attendance.

When we remarked on this, our guide told us an interesting story. Over the years, the local Indians, who lived in the hills and were pagan, and the villagers, who were mostly Catholic, had reached an informal accommodation about the use of the church. Eventually, however, the church got a hard-nosed pastor who denied use of the church for "heathen practices," and turned the Indians out. The Indians appealed to the governor, who gave the pastor an ultimatum: "Share it or lose it!" When the governor "explained" the matter that way, the pastor gave up and the church has been shared ever since. Now, many of the ceremonies are presided over by both a priest and a shaman. The Indians are not taking any chances.

These Indians were not performing human sacrifice or any other heinous or gross affronts to civilized society. In fact, these Indians are the most honest, caring, hard-working human beings imaginable. On market day, though the central square is teeming with people, you can turn your back on the market and never know it is there because it is so orderly and quiet. The Indians, although dirt poor, have a quality of happiness and serenity that is enviable in this day and age. Surely Our Parent would have welcomed these people into the church. He/She would have been displeased by the actions of the priggish pastor and supportive of the action of the governor.

I now believe that Our Parent not only does not

have a worship preference, He/She does not wish to be "worshiped" at all. If Our Parent is so powerful, our "worship" would be meaningless. We cannot add to or subtract from Our Parent's glory. Again, *we* are parents; do we wish for our children to worship us, or do we want something else? We want their respect, and we want their love, and we want something more. We want our children to be, in Maslow's words, self-actualized, and we want our children to get along with each other.

In other words, to expand Maslow's notion of "self-actualization," our fondest hope is for our children to *develop* to their greatest potential. It would be nice for them all to graduate *magna cum laude* from Harvard Medical School—and some do; but what if one of your children does and the other does not? Do you love the other less, or feel disappointment in him or her? Not if you are a "good" parent. You would not love the other less under any circumstances. You would feel disappointment only if the other falls short of being all he or she could.

The term, "development," is not synonymous with the term, "growth." Dr. Russell L. Ackoff, one of the founders and champions of the "Systems Approach," talked about the differences between them during a lecture I was fortunate enough to attend in 1985. "Growth" has to do with size and numbers. "Development" is a much more complicated notion. As he put it: "Cemeteries grow, but they do not develop." Development is more concerned with quality (of life) than quantity.

In fact, development may not have *anything* to do with quantity. We have all heard of "veddy, veddy rich" people who seem to be very unhappy because of the poor quality of their lives. They seem to go off the deep end, doing very foolish and self-destructive things in an attempt to "buy" quality. Their money might be able to buy them an environment in which a higher quality of life is possible for them, but money will not buy quality directly. Quality is a state of mind.

Ackoff pointed out that in the Middle Ages there was little need to talk of quality of life. There was *no* quality of life in most cases. Man's life was "nasty, brutish, and short," as John Hobbes captured it. The average life-span was twenty-seven years. Hardly anyone traveled more than thirty miles from home, which was in a small, disease-ridden village that offered little more than the basic needs of life, if that. The peasants who lived in those villages would have laughed at Maslow, or murdered him.

If the peasants had ever had time to ask, "What is the purpose of a life such as this?" the Church was ready with the answer: "The purpose of life is to prepare for death." Moreover, "We'll tell you how to do it." And, by the way, "We are the only ones who can; and you better listen to us because God has a terrible temper." It was not until the Crusades that hordes of men and women were exposed to other cultures, humanistic notions, and the resulting possibility that the answer to the question, "Is this all there is?" was "Not by a long shot."

V: What Our Parent Wants From Us

Okay, in some sense the purpose of life *is* to prepare for death. All of us will die. There is no getting around it. But the way to prepare for death is to develop ourselves to our fullest. Without development we are already dead. But is death the end of *development* or just the end of *biological life*? I will explore that later.

The major component of development is learning, which can be gained by a combination of study (including meditation, and prayer) and experience. In Ackoff's construct, a person can learn at three levels: informational, knowledge, and understanding.

At the informational level, for example, a detective may have command of the facts of a crime—*who, what, where, when*. At the knowledge level, the detective may be able to figure out *how* the crime was committed. The understanding level, however, requires that the detective have a firm grasp of *why* the crime was committed. *Why* is the question of motive. In fact, detectives sometimes find it easier to start from the motive—*"cherchez la femme"* (the French of course, think to look for a woman connection first) or "follow the money"—than the other way around.

The focus of our development should be understanding. Plato said that the unexamined life is not worth living, and he is right. We should not be content to know only what to do and how to do it, simply following someone else's formula; we should nurture and cherish our curiosity about the why of it.

Our children have the right idea. They ask

"Why?" and are totally put off by the parental "Because!" If you do give them a reason, and when they are young your reason is likely to be somewhat superficial, they are likely to try to explore the reason with another "Why?" No doubt about it, children have a genetic predisposition for driving parents crazy.

As our children mature, however, are we not more likely to trust them with the real reasons why? We want them to understand. We want them to seek understanding for themselves.

This is not easy. Buddhist monks spend a lifetime trying to achieve the state of understanding called "nirvana," which Webster's defines as:

> The state of perfect blessedness achieved by the extinction of individual existence and by the absorption of the soul into the supreme spirit, or by the extinction of all desires and passions.

As I understand it, the "extinction of individual existence" is not death; it is the abandonment of the idea that we have an existence totally within ourselves. I accept that, but what I find difficult to accept is that nirvana requires us to withdrawal from all earthly pleasures.

Our Parent put us in the world, and I do not believe that He/She meant it to be a "candy store" where no one is allowed to eat any of the candy. Our Parent must have meant us to enjoy the world. Our admonition to our children when we build a playroom and give them toys is: explore their possibilities, learn from them, and have fun with them, but do not abuse them or hurt each other with them. We also tell them not to get so fascinated with their toys that they forget their responsibilities, like taking out the garbage.

Also, our desires and passions are part of us. They add zest to life. Goodness is not a matter of denial; it is a matter of balance.

Ackoff's paragon of development is Robinson Crusoe. Crusoe, in the 1719 fictional story (based upon a true one) by Daniel Defoe, was shipwrecked on a tropical island with only a few supplies. Yet by using his wits and the resources available to him he managed not only to survive for many years but gain a certain quality of life in the process.

We should think of ourselves as Robinson Crusoes, put on this earth with many more resources available to us than were available to him, and therefore able to achieve a higher level of development. But we should not think of ourselves as Crusoe alone. As the poet John Donne wrote, "No man is an island." Once Crusoe found the young native whom he dubbed "Friday," Crusoe became an even more highly-developed and more fulfilled human being. We can develop better in concert with others than we can alone.

Think for a moment: whom do we know (personally or by reputation) that we would consider a paragon of development that we could emulate? Well, Christ, of course, and Mother Theresa, perhaps. But maybe we are shooting too high at first, thinking that "Gee, I could never achieve that!" and therefore not achieving much at all.

While acknowledging the magnificent development of those two, I am more struck day-to-day by some of the people I see around me who are trying to do the best they can with sometimes very slender material. Take a busboy I saw in an uncrowded restaurant in California, who was showing a waitress just how fast he could set up a table for four. He was not ordered to do that by his management, nor was there any other extrinsic reward for speed (as he stated to the unconvinced waitress). He just thought he could do it better, so he did; and he did it with pride and joy. He was a better-developed busboy than any I had ever seen. If by lack of opportunity or force of circumstance he could not be other than a busboy, he was "all that he could be." I, as a parent, would have been proud of him. I believe that is what Our Parent wants from and for us.

Maybe that sounds like a dumb example. Am I really suggesting that we ignore the Mother Theresas of the world and try to find some busboy to admire and pattern our lives after? No; what I am trying to suggest is that to develop the attitude and habit for development, we should not be afraid to start small and grow from there. One of my least favorite Christmas Carols is *The Little Drummer Boy*—but only because the infinite repetition of "pah-rum-pum-pum-pum" drives me out of my mind. The sentiment in the song is actually very good: the little drummer boy was giving God what he could, and so should we.

Ackoff equated "development" with "quality."

V: What Our Parent Wants From Us

But how does one define "quality?" Ackoff did not; he told stories and let us conclude for ourselves what quality is. I told a "quality" story about the busboy. Can we do better?

Robert Pirsig tried very hard to define quality in his profound philosophical book called *Zen and the Art of Motorcycle Maintenance* (1974), but, in the end, quite cheerfully failed:

> Quality...you know what it is, yet you don't know what it is. But that's self-contradictory. But some things *are* better than others, that is, they have more quality. But when you try to say what the quality is, apart from the things that have it, it all goes *poof*! There's nothing to talk about. But if you can't say what Quality is, how do you know what it is or how do you know that it even exists? If no one knows what it is, then for all practical purposes it doesn't exist at all. But for all practical purposes it really *does* exist. What else are the grades based on? Why else would people pay fortunes for some things and throw others in the trash pile? Obviously some things are better than others...but what's the "betterness"?...So round and round you go, spinning mental wheels and nowhere finding anyplace to get traction. What the hell is Quality? What *is* it?

Pirsig, like everyone else, has been reduced to stories. In fact, his whole book was really a story about quality.

But what is wrong with that? We can either spend our lives wondering what development/

quality is, or we can develop. So how can we develop fully? How do we learn to "understand?"

Certainly we can benefit from individual study (yes, of stories too), meditation and prayer. But these alone would ignore the real benefits of sharing the fruits of our study, meditation and prayer with others.

Organized religions purport to do this but, in my (admittedly limited) experience, many are overloaded with things that get in the way: hierarchy and other manifestations of power; unwieldy and rigid dogmas; a tendency to structure everything into set-piece rites and ceremonies; and a bunch of sin-based rules. The times I have truly felt a kinship to Our Parent in concert with others were when I and a few friends got together in one of their basements and we just sort of "rapped" about our relationship to God. The Catholic Church started out that way; maybe it just got too big.

Another way we can learn to develop is by real prayer: having conversations with Our Parent, without worrying about the words; invoking His/Her participation in everything we do, not just in our problems. Do we not call our earthly parents routinely, just to hear their voices and to keep them informed about our lives through good times and bad?

Trying to get help with problems is okay too, but I believe we need to be somewhat careful about it. Beseeching is not a substitute for thinking and acting on your own. As a father myself, I do not mind helping my son through a problem; but I do somewhat resent it when my son presents me with a problem that he was just too lazy to think through himself. I much prefer something like: "Dad, I've got a problem. Here's what I have thought and done about it, but I seem to be stuck." I want my son to get to the point where he solves more and more of his problems without help from me. That is not cold-heartedness on my part; that is development on his. Our Parent may prefer to have us approach problems like that also.

Another way we can learn to develop is to observe how our fellow humans are doing it. If Our Parent is able to help *us* to develop, He/She must be helping *others* also. Learning from others can have the same benefit as trying to learn directly from Our Parent. Even if others do nothing else for us directly, they can help us raise our sights. The "four-minute mile" was impossible until Roger Bannister did it. Now all of the top milers are doing it in much less. Zebulon Pike once proclaimed that the mountain peak later to be named after him would be forever unclimbable. Now people run marathons up and down Pike's Peak, sometimes more than one in succession. We need to learn how much it is possible to develop.

We can also develop by performing acts that encourage development: helping people, doing community service, even, as the bumper stickers say, engaging in random and senseless acts of kindness.

I have mentioned several times that Our Parent

can help us develop, but it is important to consider the framework within which that help can be given. There are limitations.

VI: Some Limitations of Our Parent

What? Our Parent, creator of the universe, with limitations? How can that be? Isn't Our Parent perfect? The answer is that Our Parent can have limitations and still be perfect (I will try to explain). Also, were it not for these limitations, our lives and our ability to develop would be substantially different. And the limitations are inextricably linked together. They have to do with *free will*, the *nature of the universe* and *time*.

If we do not have free will, then we cannot be held accountable for anything bad or be given credit for anything good. Without free will, this whole exercise is pointless. But by granting us free will, Our Parent accepts a stunning limitation. When a human being says "No" to Our Parent, for that instant their power is at least equal.

Free will is at the same time the greatest gift and the greatest challenge to the human race. It is the greatest gift because it opens the door for the kind of mature relationship with Our Parent that is so fervently to be desired. It is also the door to true development. But it is the greatest challenge because it carries the possibility that we can foul it all up through our own fault. It is up to us to accept the gift and the challenge in the proper spirit.

But free will leads to the second limitation. Our Parent had several choices for running the universe. For one, He/She could have chosen to run every aspect of the universe in real time, hands on (figuratively speaking, of course). At first thought, that seems to be the view expressed by Jesus in Matthew 10/29, *New American Standard Bible*: "Are not two sparrows sold for a cent? And yet not one of them will fall to the ground apart from your Father." But the sense of the passage is tricky. It may mean that Our Parent *notices and cares about* even the fall of two sparrows without causing or controlling it. That interpretation puts Our Parent more in the *Daddy/Mommy* camp, so I like it better. A total control interpretation, however, means that Our Parent would be directly responsible for *everything*, even *calamities*, and thus could fairly be blamed for every specific tornado, plague, and every form of natural disaster and human affliction. I do not believe Our Parent would deliberately treat His/Her children that way.

Another way to run the universe would be to have it self-running, based upon deterministic laws. Sir Isaac Newton (1642-1727), the most towering scientific figure of his—some would say, *any*—age, looked around him at the order in the universe and concluded that the universe was a machine—not *like* a machine—a machine. The planets revolved around the sun in a predictable and repeatable path as an extension of the mathematics of an apple falling on your head. As Isaac Asimov described it in his book, *Understanding Physics* (1966):

> From the vast universe down to the tiniest components thereof, all might be looked on as obeying the same laws of mechanics by physical interaction as do the familiar machines of everyday life....

The universe of Newton was totally deterministic by any measure. A reasonable definition of a deterministic model is found on *Biology Online*: "a mathematical model in which the parameters and variables are not subject to random fluctuations, so that the system is at any time entirely defined by the initial conditions chosen." Cause leads to effect; effect becomes another cause. But since we are part of the universe we are affected by its laws. If the molecules in our brains were lined up according to deterministic laws, what choices would we really have? Our destiny would have been settled at the moment of conception—actually, even before the first amphibian crawled out of the primordial ooze. We could not have "random" thoughts. We would not have control of our own actions.

But the Newtonian universe prevailed for about 200 years until along came Einstein and his colleagues to turn this deterministic model on its ear. As Isaac Asimov continues:

> ...And yet by the end of the [nineteenth] century, the Newtonian view had been found to be mere-

ly an approximation. The universe was more complicated than it seemed. Broader and subtler explanations for its workings had to be found.

When I wrote the First Edition eleven years ago, I thought I had the answer. Albert Einstein, in a very famous statement, said that he did not believe that God would "play dice with the universe." But, in fact, the theories of Einstein are heavily dependent upon quantum theory, first formulated in 1900 by a German Physicist, Max Planck. In quantum theory, a watershed between classic physics and modern physics, nearly all physical properties and processes are governed by probability.

Let's use the rolling dice example (with apologies to Einstein). In rolling a pair of dice there is only one way to roll a two: that is with a one on one die and a one on the other. On the other hand, there are a number of ways to roll a seven: e.g., a six and a one; a one and a six; a five and a two; a two and a five; and so on. If the dice are not loaded and the roll is fair, one ought to expect a whole lot more sevens than twos. In fact, if over a thousand rolls or so one gets a lot more twos than sevens, it is easy (and correct) to say that the dice or the rolls are not fair. Over a large number of rolls, the percentages of twos and sevens (and all the other possible numbers) can be predicted with great precision. One should not think that the laws of probability are weak and not to be trusted. They work very well.

That is the way I believed the universe works. Molecules bounce around at random, mostly rolling sevens—representing their most stable state—but once in a while they roll a two, and do something unexpected. There is a finite probability that all the molecules of air will gather in the corner of the room with the result that everyone in the room will suffocate. It does not happen because the most likely distribution of molecules is uniform, equally scattered within the space available.

Going beyond molecules, we speak of the laws of probability governing the occurrence of rain and earthquakes, the gender of a child, and the number of auto accidents over the Fourth of July weekend. These things are set and no outside force is required to keep them going. In fact, these things will continue to follow the laws of probability unless acted on by an outside force. We can seed clouds to get more rain; we may be able to influence the gender of a child (I'm not sure we can yet); we can decide not to drive over the Fourth of July weekend. In the overwhelming majority of cases, however, these things are self-running.

But then I had a paralyzing thought. What I have just described is not randomness in the true sense, but simply determinism in complex systems. It has to do more with our inability to measure and predict than with the processes themselves. A deterministic model is a probabilistic model where the probability is one.

Let's go back to the example of a roll of the dice. The action is so complex that we cannot truly measure the input conditions. The position of the dice in the hand, the amount of sweat on the palm, the density of the air, the friction of the felt surface, the speed of the throw, how the dice are let go, how high the dice are when they leave the hand, gravitational variations, the initial spin, and probably dozens of other factors make it impossible to predict the final outcome of any particular throw. So we give up on doing that and settle for results in the aggregate. We use probabilistic models and formulas to calculate those results, but each individual result would be predictable if we knew all of the input conditions and had a computer powerful enough to do the calculations.

So the probabilistic model does not support the idea of free will either. It helps, but we're not there yet. We can imagine Our Parent having a big enough computer. What we need is some true randomness that even Our Parent can't get around. But at this time I felt really stuck, with nowhere to go.

Then I discovered what might be Our Parent's greatest achievement. No, not creating order out of chaos; creating chaos out of order.

Most people by now are aware of the new science of Chaos Theory through the phenomenon of the "Butterfly Effect." From Wikipedia, an internet encyclopedia:

> The term "butterfly effect" itself is related to the work of Edward Lorenz, based in Chaos Theory and sensitive dependence on initial conditions, first described in the literature by Jacques Hadamard in 1890 and popularized by Pierre

Duhem's 1906 book. The idea that one butterfly could have a far-reaching ripple effect on subsequent events seems first to have appeared in a 1952 short story by Ray Bradbury about time travel, although Lorenz made popular the term. In 1961, Lorenz was using a numerical computer model to rerun a weather prediction, when, as a shortcut on a number in the sequence, he entered the decimal .506 instead of entering the full .506127 the computer would hold. The result was a completely different weather scenario. Lorenz published his findings in a 1963 paper for the New York Academy of Sciences noting that "One meteorologist remarked that if the theory were correct, one flap of a seagull's wings could change the course of weather forever." Later speeches and papers by Lorenz used the more poetic butterfly. According to Lorenz, upon failing to provide a title for a talk he was to present at the 139th meeting of the American Association for the Advancement of Science in 1972, Philip Merilees concocted *Does the flap of a butterfly's wings in Brazil set off a tornado in Texas.*

But that was just a result of extreme input sensitivity. Small perturbations could result in large changes downstream. In my opinion, the important result of research in Chaos Theory is the discovery that *there are no truly deterministic systems past a certain point.* Even in simple systems like pendulums, when the system was pushed too far, the mathematical equation that described its motion went from linear to nonlinear. As James Gleick put it in his seminal book, *Chaos: Making a New Science*: "Those studying chaotic dynamics discovered that the disorderly behavior of simple systems acted as a creative process. It generated complexity..." A creative process denies total determinism and allows for the exercise of free will. Even though we have learned that there are patterns to chaos, there is enough looseness to light and fan the creative spark.

Thus the real beauty of the universe is that it allows for both stability and creativity. Determinism is a special case of probability theory; probability theory is a special case of Chaos theory. True creativity is not possible in a deterministic world. Stability is not possible in a totally chaotic world.

But in managing the universe through a wonderful mixture of stability and chaos, and granting mankind free will, Our Parent has given up an incredible power and accepted a stunning limitation. He/She is no longer in control. The universe is self-running.

A third limitation of Our Parent is not really a limitation at all, but an acknowledgment of the way things are. We speak of God as being unbounded by *time*: that time is meaningless to God; that God lives in the Past, the Present, and the Future. Thus we say that God knows the future.

But as a good parent yourself, would you let your child go on a camping trip if you were absolutely certain that your child would be killed and eaten by a bear? I am just as certain that you would not. In fact, unless you were very sure that the probabilities of such were very low, you would not even entertain the idea. No way! End of discussion! Would Our Parent act any differently? I think not.

If we as earthly parents would not expose our children in that way, how can we explain the failure of our "Perfect Parent" to protect us from natural and man-made calamities? The way out of the dilemma is to consider two notions: that the laws of the universe are a mixture of deterministic, probabilistic and chaotic (which I have already discussed); and that knowing the future is a contradiction in terms. Having invented time, Our Parent is now bound by it. The future is not available, even to Our Parent, until it happens. There is no such thing as a square circle. There is no such thing as the occurrence of a future event that has not occurred. That is not a limitation of the Deity; it is a limitation of the concept itself.

All of us can guess at the outcome of a future event, and if the laws of probability (I will use that as shorthand for all three states from now on.) are on our side, some of those guesses can be mighty good. But the favorite does not always win the Kentucky Derby. Our Parent is an infinitely better guesser, but if the laws of probability and chaos really pertain, He/She cannot predict the outcome of every event with certainty.

This answers the awful conundrum that goes something like: If Our Parent knew what Hitler would do to the world, why would He/She allow Hitler to be born? My rejoinder is that Our Parent did *not* know. Our Parent set the world in motion under probabilistic control. Hitler was born and was allowed to make his own choices in accordance with the dictates of his own free will.

Why then, when Our Parent discovered what Hitler was up to, did not Our Parent get rid of him, or at least neutralize him. My response is that for that to happen through a human agent (by way of assassination, perhaps) would have violated the free will of the human agent. For that to happen through a natural agent, such as a bolt of lightning, would have violated the laws of probability.

This gets tougher when one considers that the laws of probability sometimes result in pain to the innocent, such as when a child contracts leukemia. But disease is not a punishment, such was thought in ages past (and in some religions today), it is an accident: it is the dice turning up a two. When it happens, the good human parent tries to compensate for the affliction with additional love and tenderness. Our Parent surely must do the same thing.

So what about miracles? We suppose that Our Parent can do anything He/She wants to. Can't Our Parent make an exception once in a while for a worthy cause, monumental or trivial? In Rev Tevye's wonderful song from *Fidder on the Roof*, the harassed character asks God: "Would it spoil some vast eternal plan if I were a wealthy man?" My uncle was very devout until, when he was still a young man, his beloved dog became very ill. With tears in his eyes, my uncle promised God all sorts of good deeds if only He would save his little friend. When the dog died, my uncle turned his back on God for the rest of his life. In each case, God was apparently silent, even though a favorable intervention in neither event was likely to have turned the cosmos all atumble.

How about something more substantial? A tornado is heading into town and the townspeople take refuge in a church which is then struck by the tornado and everyone inside is killed. Couldn't Our Parent have made an exception there? If the tornado had missed the church, many would have called it a miracle and the number of worshipers would have tripled in a fortnight. Was it really a miracle? Since, in this example, the tornado hit the church anyway even though everyone inside was praying like mad, should we conclude that Our Parent was indifferent, leaving the rest of us confused and resentful? Or, as in less enlightened days, that God (or the gods) was angry and craved a fresh supply of virgins?

I have come to believe that Our Parent does not perform miracles, in the sense of *physical* interventions. The laws of probability sometimes demonstrate better-than-expected outcomes, but these are natural and within the skirts, albeit on the edges, of normal probability distributions. Very sick people sometimes get well. A tornado will depart from its predicted trajectory and miss the church. Our Parent deserves neither direct credit nor direct blame.

What about *indirect* blame? A tougher question to answer is that if Our Parent is so powerful, why did He/She make the universe with so many flaws that bad calamities happen to good people. Couldn't the range of probabilities have been made tighter such that aberrant events and conditions like children's leukemia and church-destroying tornadoes would never occur in the first place? Couldn't He/She have squashed the Brazilian butterfly while it was still a caterpillar?

For me, at least a partial answer takes me back to the idea that the purpose of life is development. I contend that in a perfect world there would be no opportunity or stimulus for development. Life must have challenges or no one would grow. We can argue about how much challenge is enough, of course. Clearly, some people's lives are indeed "nasty, brutish and short" whereas others' are (on the surface at least) quite wonderful. Does the greater challenge faced by the former lead to greater development, or does the increased hardship force them into the lower tier of Maslow's Pyramid (survival) and keep them there? Does the extra time and decreased pressure enjoyed by the latter automatically help them achieve "self-actualization" and greater development? Hard to say. The world is as it is and, at this point at least, we have to accept that Our Parent at least has tried to set the right balance.

Does Our Parent ever respond to our prayers and intervene in the affairs of mankind? But wait: first we have to consider how we even are able to communicate with Our Parent. What is the medium for petition and response? Is it literally "our mouths to God's ear," or something else?

If Our Parent does not perform physical interventions, the medium would not involve the five

VI: Some Limitations of Our Parent

physical senses. Well, surely you have had the experience of thoughts appearing in your head without your willing them there. We can be in a sense-free environment, as in a deep cave, yet we can be flooded with images and ideas. We also have dreams that leap into our semi-consciousness seemingly unbidden. It makes sense to me that all this is related to the phenomenon of intuition, which Wikipedia states is: "understanding without apparent effort, quick and ready insight seemingly independent of previous experiences or empirical knowledge." Where does intuition come from? Perhaps some of it comes from Our Parent. If so, then we can think of an "intuition channel" that is able to carry messages back and forth between ourselves and Our Parent without recourse to the physical realm.

So we can pray using the "intuition channel;" but will Our Parent listen and respond? Yes, if we pray the right sort of prayer. No, if we are asking for a physical miracle. My uncle stopped believing in God because God did not answer his prayer. If he had understood Our Parents' limitations—inevitable results of allowing free will, building a probabilistic universe, and not knowing the future—rather than asking God to save his dog (requiring a miracle), my uncle should have asked God to help him get through the bad time he was having and to help him cope if his dog did not recover. The people in the church should not have prayed for God to turn away the tornado but to ask His/Her help in facing the situation and its aftermath.

The intuition channel *could* be used by Our Parent to produce physical results because, clearly, once in our conscious or subconscious—thoughts and dreams are capable of producing physical responses such as sexual arousal, adrenaline flow for fight-or-flight, tears or laughs, perhaps even healing or lack of it. Perhaps some or all of those outcomes would not violate Our Parents self-imposed limitations.

But, in general, we should pray for and expect help on things that do not require miraculous physical interventions.

Here's a tricky one. Let's say that we are in daily communication with Our Parent and making good moral choices, couldn't we at least expect some *warning* from Our Parent through the intuition channel about an impending difficulty or danger? In the First Edition, I allowed that Our Parent could save you from getting hit by a bus by warning you of danger. Here was an "out" concerning the free will limitation. As in the motto of Fox News, Our Parent would only present; you would decide to jump back or not. But even that, I believe now, would violate the laws of probability. And it would require a decision on Our Parent's part as to whom to save and whom not to, and this might violate the "love all His/Her children the same" principle. So I don't believe we can expect any divine warnings.

So what kind of help *can* we expect from Our Parent, and how can we get it? We're right back to development. We should pray for help to reach higher and to avoid the things that hold us back. We should expect to receive guidance in shaping our conscience, avoiding temptation, making life choices, coping with disaster, or solving a problem, as examples. Many beneficial interventions are available beyond physical miracles. We get this help through the "intuition channel." All we have to do is ask for it.

But there are a few caveats. As my daughter points out, not everything coming down the intuition channel comes from Our Parent; we have to be "tuned in." But when we are struggling with a problem and we ask for Our Parent's help, He/She can intervene through the intuitive pathway without violating the laws of probability or free will. He/She can listen to us, encourage us, and plant ideas for our consideration. Free will is not violated, because the person does not have to pay attention to the input or idea. Probability is not violated because the intervention is not physical.

Here is another caveat. Because of free will, not only do we have the option of ignoring Our Parent's suggestions given to us through (using a computer analogy) the "Intuition Internet," we also control the connection. If we fail to hook up our spiritual "modem," or fail to keep it in good repair, we will not have access to the on-line guidance Our Parent is so willing to give us.

Moreover, remember the old adage: "God helps those who help themselves?" This common-sense saying is very much in the spirit of the relationship we are trying to establish and nurture with Our Parent. We should, at least, begin by trying to solve our problems ourselves, because that is the way we develop. On the other hand, we should not delay seeking help from Our Parent until a miracle is required, because then it may be too late. Our Parent may be constrained by the laws of probability and free will that have been in place since the creation of the universe.

Finally, we need to pay attention to a good response when one is given. Suppose a young man loves a young woman but, alas, his love is unrequited; so he asks Our Parent to melt her cold, cold heart. As already discussed, this is the wrong sort of prayer. For Our Parent to comply might require interfering with the girl's free will, or giving her a divine aphrodisiac, so no go. But even though it's the wrong kind of prayer, Our Parent may be willing to suggest—through the intuition channel again—that the girl was not suitable for him. (I'm sure Our Parent would not expect the young man's gratitude right away...)

And that anecdote shows that physical outcomes are not totally denied from interventions by Our Parent; they will just be indirect. If the young man accepted the divine suggestion to stop pursuing her, all sorts of physical outcomes ensue, including perhaps even averting the birth of a child. And we know that a patient's attitude can sometimes make all the difference. The placebo effect, wherein a subject/patient is given a phony pill ("placebo") instead of a real one, will sometimes show all the effects of having been given the genuine article. So we may consider where a doctor's "miracle" cure might come from. Is it because of the medicine/surgery or because of the strong faith of the patient (perhaps encouraged by Our Parent) that the medicine/surgery will work? The mind can communicate with Our Parent; Our Parent can communicate to the body through the mind.

Given Our Parent's limitations, does this mean that we should not ask Our Parent for miracles? Well, yes and no. We should ask Our Parent to help us. We may not know whether the help requires a miracle or not. But we should accept the answer, whatever it is, with good grace. We should not interpret the lack of a positive response as a personal rejection. Our Parent may have been bound by the constraints.

So we should continue to pray and ask Our Parent for what we need. Whatever happens, we should thank Our Parent for listening and be comforted by the idea that Our Parent feels as badly as we do about what, for us, is a seemingly poor outcome. Is this not the way it works with earthly parents?

So far, I have discussed the notion of development as unencumbered by any obstacles. Are there any? Sure there are. It is one way to describe sin.

VII: Sin as Obstacle to Development

If Our Parent has limitations on His/Her ability to help us develop, more important are the limitations we place on ourselves. One of these is sin. The more an action or thought process interferes with our development, and therefore our relationship with Our Parent, the worse the sin.

But that's not the traditional view of sin. My ancient *Webster's New World Dictionary* has a definition of sin as follows: "the breaking of a religious law or a moral principle, especially through a willful act." This definition is okay as far as it goes, but it is not of much help in what I am trying to convey here. First, I am trying to stay away from legalistic concerns, such as existing religious law, and discuss sin as it affects our relationship with Our Parent. Second, I believe we need to consider sins of *omission* as well as those of *commission*.

In Catholic dogma, all of us are born in sin, the legacy of the Original Sin committed by Adam and Eve in the Garden of Eden. Because of this sin (the story goes), God sent His only begotten Son to redeem us. Even with Christ's sacrifice on the cross, we still need the Sacrament of Baptism to purify us.

The Sacrament can be administered by anyone, priest or not, Catholic or not, by a sprinkling of water on a person's forehead, accompanied by the words: "I baptize thee in the name of the Father, the Son, and the Holy Spirit." A person can also be baptized by martyrdom (Baptism of Blood) and by leading a good life (Baptism of Desire).

As a child, I was taught how to administer the sacrament in case I was ever at the scene of an accident or other situation in which a person wished to be baptized (or not; the person might be unconscious) and no priest was available. I was also taught that an infant who died without being baptized was not allowed into God's heaven. Instead, the little innocent, whose only sin was the sin of Adam and Eve, would go to a place of "natural happiness" (whatever that was) called *Limbo*.

To me, all of this violates the Good Parent test. A Good Parent would simply not operate that way. I believe that we all start off with a clean slate. We are all, as only the Virgin Mary and Christ were supposed to be, conceived without sin. We sin only when we exercise our free will in improper ways. For whatever reason Christ died, it was not to redeem us from Original Sin.

As an aside, this book is not meant to be an essay on the shortcomings of the Catholic Church. I know more about the Catholic Church because I was raised that way, and therefore most of my examples of things that do not make sense to me are taken from that source. But there are things that disturb me about other religions as well, and that is why I keep returning to the standard of the Good Parent. I would have a problem with any religious proviso, dogma, teaching, or practice that violates that standard.

Original Sin is only the beginning (no pun intended). There exists a whole catalogue of sins, the seriousness of each, and the prescribed punishment. The Catholic Church has only recently revised the catalogue.

The most serious sins are *mortal* sins—the punishment for these is everlasting hell. The only way to avoid punishment for these is through the Sacrament of Penance (now called Reconciliation) usually administered face-to-face with a priest in the Confessional, accompanied by true contrition and a heartfelt promise not to commit the sin again. Under some circumstances, group absolution can be given. If a person is dying and no priest is available, a sincere Act of Contrition is enough.

The least serious are *venial* sins. A person can "work off" the punishment for these in life by Confession and Absolution, by good works, and by the granting of *Indulgences*. (One of the things so upsetting to Martin Luther and the other reformers was that the Church was selling *Indulgences* to fill its coffers.) If a person has not worked off all the punishment earned, the person goes to Purgatory, a place of temporary punishment, before being let into heaven.

I have no problem with the *fact* of sin. Some sins can be very ugly and harmful to society and harmful

VII: Sin as Obstacle to Development

to our relationship with Our Parent. Clearly there must be deterrents to sin, and punishments (or rehabilitation; more later) for the sinner. Where I have the problem is *overemphasis* on sin, shame, and guilt.

The Ten Commandments from the Old Testament are an excellent guide to human conduct, but they are unbalanced. There are only two "Shalts" (Honor your Father and Mother; Keep Holy the Sabbath Day), but eight "Shalt Nots" (Have Strange Gods before Me; Take the Name of the Lord thy God in Vain; Kill; Commit Adultery; Steal; Bear False Witness Against Thy Neighbor; Covet Thy Neighbor's Wife; and Covet Thy Neighbor's Goods).

Actually, the Ten Commandments we see hung in federal and state buildings (although some may be taken down after the recent Supreme Court rulings) are products of a little shorthand. The First Commandment is usually stated as: "I am the Lord thy God; thou shalt not have other gods before me." (Exodus 20) What is left out is the rest of the text: "for I the Lord thy God am a jealous God, visiting the iniquity of the fathers upon the children unto the third and fourth generation of those that hate me." Yes, and this passage is followed by: "and showing mercy unto thousands of them that love me, and keep my commandments." But once again, the Bible shows us a God who punishes innocents even beyond the ones who directly commit the sin. A God to fear, not a God to love.

Interestingly, in the New Testament, Christ is

reported to have reduced the Ten Commandments to just two, both positive: "Love God with your whole heart, your whole mind, and your whole soul;" and "Love your neighbor as yourself."

The problem with sin-based rules is that they focus too much on the negative. We should be focusing on the positive. Sports teams know what happens when they play not to lose rather than play to win. What happens is that they do not play at all and lose because of it.

In golf or tennis, one of the secrets to a good game is to imagine the perfectly hit shot and try to make it, not allowing yourself to dwell on what might happen if you don't make it.

As human parents, we tend to focus on the negative way too much. Little Johnny comes home from school with five "A's" on his report card and two "C's." Do we rejoice at the "A's" or ask him why in the world he got two stinking "C's?" He better start studying more. And, by the way, his room is a filthy mess. How does Johnny feel? Is he more motivated to get better grades and to keep his room clean, or does he sigh and say, "What's the use?"

If Our Parent is the "Good Parent," He/She will focus on the positive. Our Parent will encourage us to keep trying, to take some satisfaction from our successes, and not to get too downhearted if we stumble once in a while.

We should not think of ourselves as *sinners*, poor weak fools that are unworthy to be in the company of the God of Justice. We are *learners*, who will not

VII: Sin as Obstacle to Development

always do everything right, and Our Parent knows this and wants to stay near us to help us do better.

As a friend suggested at breakfast the other day, the most effective way to learn is through experience, and we gain the most experience through failure. Perhaps we need to sin to learn. Saint Augustine (354-430 AD), somewhat of a libertine as a young man, is reported to have prayed: "Save me, Oh Lord, but not yet!" Once "saved," Augustine became one of the most distinguished fathers of the Church. Perhaps his earlier sinful life was necessary for the intensity of his devotion later. Obviously, one could take that too far, but it is an interesting thought.

Although we need to focus on the positive, the subject of sin is still worth some discussion. In my view, as stated before, we sin when we act or fail to act in a way such that we have a negative effect on the relationship with Our Parent. The greater the negative effect, the greater the sin.

The way we can have the greatest negative effect on the relationship with Our Parent is through abuse of His/Her other children, our brothers and sisters. Remember how it distresses you when your children fight?

We have to remember that Our Parent loves His/Her children equally. Probably all children ask their parents the question: "Who do you love the best?" My father had a neat answer for the three of us. I was my father's "favorite oldest son;" my sister was my father's "favorite daughter;" and our little brother was my father's "favorite youngest son."

I'm sure Our Parent would have the same kind of answer for us. Since He/She loves us equally, Our Parent would hate to see us doing something to gain unfair advantage over one another. Using our gift of free will in killing each other, stealing from each other, hurting each other, being envious of each other, failing to help each other, being prejudiced against each other, being unjust with each other, or simply being unkind to each other: all would displease Our Parent and cause our relationship to suffer.

Being kind to people is the real secret to a good relationship with Our Parent. When you are kind to people, you listen to them, help them if you can, and treat them with the respect they deserve as fellow children of Our Parent. All of the "sins" described above start with violations of the "kindness" principle.

The best arbiter of sin is a healthy conscience. Of course, a conscience can be overdeveloped to the point that a person goes around afraid and guilt-ridden thinking everything he or she does (and what everybody else does) is wrong. A conscience can be underdeveloped to the point that a person thinks that nothing he or she does is wrong. Pathologies exist at both ends. In my attempt to accentuate the positive, a conscience—to be truly healthy—should include an increasing ability to recognize development opportunities, not just faults.

A healthy conscience would also be somewhat flexible with the application of moral principles—not

VII: Sin as Obstacle to Development

with the principles themselves, but the application of them. Moral principles can collide. What then? For example, one should not lie, but one should also be kind. Is it a sin to lie out of kindness? How do we develop the good judgment that can add wisdom to the conscience we were born with?

Let's go back to the parent/child analogy. We tell our children "that's good," "that's bad," "do you know how what you just did makes me feel?" It's one of your jobs as a parent to help shape the little conscience.

In fact, all of us come equipped with what Eric Berne, the developer of Transactional Analysis, calls the "Parent Tapes," which are the legacy of our earthly parents, and which become part of our personality in life. Ian Mitroff, in his book, *Stakeholders of the Organizational Mind* (1983), paraphrases Berne this way:

> The Parent embodies two distinct clusters of attributes. We can say also that the character of the Parent is bifurcated, or contains two sub-characters: a nurturing or protective Parent and a critical or judging Parent. The protective Parent is basically nourishing and supportive. It provides the foundation for the development of the individual as a healthy ego. The critical Parent, however, serves no less a necessary role. If the Parent were wholly nourishing, then the individual would never become separate, that is, an autonomous individual.

Please note that the "Parent" of the quote is Eric

Berne's term for what Sigmund Freud called the *superego*, and not what I have been calling "Our Parent," which is my new term for God. Confused?

Well, what I meant in quoting Berne is that our healthy conscience as adults is the result of two inputs. The first is what we get from the Parent Tapes. If the "tapes" are of high quality—if we feel protected and nurtured, and at the same time we have a good understanding of right and wrong—then chances are our conscience starts out healthy. Conversely, we can start out with a conscience warped by an unwholesome or uncaring upbringing. We owe it to our children (and also to Our Parent) to do as good a job as we can here.

The second input to our conscience is what we add to it as adults. We can start out with a healthy conscience and improve it or corrupt it. One of our oft-repeated discussions with Our Parent should be aimed at improving the health of our conscience. The other way to avoid corrupting our conscience is to avoid corrupting influences. If we do something "bad" often enough, we become inured to it and no longer think of it as bad.

To sum up, a sin is something a healthy conscience tells you is likely to harm the relationship between you and Our Parent. Your over-developed conscience can tell you that something is a sin when it really is not. Logic might say that if you think something is a sin then it is a sin. But would Our Parent condemn you for something trivial just because you thought it was more important than it was? I think not.

On the other hand, your underdeveloped conscience might persuade you that something is not a sin when it really is. In this case, I believe that Our Parent would condemn you for it if He/She judged that you could have known the difference, but just did not bother to think upon it enough; or that your life style had clouded your judgment.

I have discussed sin, but I have posited no afterlife consequences. Come to think of it, I have not discussed any afterlife rewards for good behavior either. Let's fix that.

VIII: Afterlife: Reward & Punishment

On a whimsical note, a distant cousin of mine, James Branch Cabell, a famous writer at the beginning of the twentieth century, thought that both heaven and hell were illusions. His mystical tale, *Jurgen* (1919), renders Cabell's exposition in a humorous way.

Like Dante searching for Beatrice, the hero, Jurgen, went off to look for his missing wife in many realms, including heaven and hell. Interviewing God (who was surrounded by all sorts of angels), Jurgen was surprised to learn that heaven was simply a place God had invented to preserve the illusions of Jurgen's grandmother. There, all was sweetness and light. Jurgen, although in reality by this time a cynical fifty-something pawnbroker, was the little boy his grandmother remembered him to be.

Interviewing "Grandfather Satan," who was in charge of coming up with ever more severe and innovative punishments for those in the nether regions, Jurgen learned that hell, on the other hand, had been created to preserve the illusions of Jurgen's forefathers:

VIII: Afterlife: Reward & Punishment

> For they were exceedingly proud of their sins. And Koschei [Cabell's Supreme Being, who "made things as they are"] happened to notice Earth once upon a time, with your forefathers walking about it in the enormity of their sins and in the terrible punishments they expected in requital...after he had his laugh out, he created Hell extempore, and made it just such a place as your forefathers imagined it to be, in order to humor the pride of your forefathers.

By the way, by applying the Good Parent standard, it is difficult to conceive that Our Parent would have unleashed so formidable a being as Satan on the Earth. People get in enough trouble simply by making bad choices in the exercise of their free will. Would the Good Parent really make life that much harder for His/Her children? I have a hard time with that. I believe that Satan is an invention of man (another myth, if you like) to act as an excuse for some of our weaknesses ("The Devil made me do it!").

Another traditional part both of our earthly life and of the afterlife involves angels. Whatever angels are (if angels exist) I have a difficult time believing that they are as man-centered as the Bible and tradition make them out to be. The notion of "guardian" angels—in the Catholic tradition, at least, each person is assigned a guardian angel by God, whose major function is to watch over that person for his/her lifetime—seems particularly to be a product of man's arrogance. In any case, my Good Parent standard fails me here, so I will not comment on angels further.

Let's go back to the discussion about reward and punishment. What is the reward for "being all that you can be" in whatever life you have and what is the punishment for failure? Mohammed, writing in the Koran, was very explicit. Although some very pious and believing women would undoubtedly be eligible for entry, clearly the Paradise Mohammed describes is for men. From Will Durant's book, *The Age of Faith* (1950), comes the following condensed description:

> ...there will be virgins "never yet touched by man or jinn [author's note: jinn were spirits, most of whom were bad, having very human characteristics and spending most of their time getting human beings into mischief], ...in beauty like the jacinth and coral stone...with swelling bosoms and modest gaze, with eyes as fair and pure as sheltered eggs," and bodies made of musk, and free from the imperfections and indignities of mortal flesh. Each blessed male will have seventy-two of these houris for his reward, and neither age nor weariness nor death shall mar the loveliness of these maidens, or their comrades' bliss.

Pretty enticing. This promise of a Paradise that everyone (well, men anyway) could relate to, plus the doctrine of predestination, in which "no danger could hasten, nor any caution defer, the predestined hour of death," has made Muslim warriors willing, and even eager, to take awful chances on the battlefield.

In fact, this whole idea has taken a rather nasty

turn. Whereas once we might have smirked at this notion of heaven, recently we have experienced chilling demonstrations that the promise of an eternal reward can motivate a legion of suicide bombers—even women. The Palestinian Jihad, the events of 9/11/01, the takeover by the Taliban in Afghanistan, and the murderous assassinations in Iraq have all taken place since the First Edition of this book.

Mohammed's idea of hell was pretty explicit also, conjuring up all sorts of physical and mental tortures. But most of us do not have an explicit view of an afterlife reward. From common folklore we get pictures of angels, harps, clouds, and golden light. We seem to be much more able to describe the agonies of hell. We speak of heaven as being in the presence of God, but we do not know what that means exactly and, frankly, that sort of heaven does not seem all that appealing. Mark Twain once remarked that some place he had visited was "like heaven without all the boring music." Our view of heaven with angels, harps and such is, well, not very exciting. Emily Dickenson contrasted the incredible ecstasy of *Wild Nights— Wild Nights* with her lover and eternally "rowing in Eden."

I find it hard to fathom a heaven where all we do is bask in the presence of Our Parent, transfixed by His/Her beauty. That is way too passive. Humans are much more active. We generally have to be doing something to feel happy and fulfilled. And we seem to demand more and more participation in things. We are warming to interactive TV. When we go to rock concerts, we can't just sit there; we have to leap about with our hands clapping far above our head. It is hard to imagine that all that will change when we get to heaven and that Our Parent would expect us to be thrilled by it.

A friend of mine had an interesting thought. One of the lessons he took from *Genesis* was that man would not be happy with God alone. After all, Adam (Chapter 2, not Chapter 1, which has a different sequence) was alone with God in the Garden of Eden until God, perhaps reacting to Adam's loneliness, decided: "It is not good that man should be alone; I will make him a help mate for him." Birds and beasts followed, but Adam was unsatisfied until God had taken one of Adam's ribs and made Eve. My friend believes *Genesis* to be literal truth and concludes that heaven would not be heaven without his wife. (Knowing his wife, I understand what he means. His wife is a wonderful person and they are very much in love. They cannot fathom separation even in death.) I believe that this part of the Bible is myth, but I take from *Genesis* that I am not the only one who cannot imagine an afterlife in isolation from everyone but God.

But is there an afterlife at all? What would be the purpose of an afterlife: motivator, deterrent, a settling of accounts, compensation, retribution? To get to the answer, I believe we must go back to two notions: the nature of Our Parent; and the purpose of life in the first place. There has to be an afterlife:

because a Good Parent would always want His/Her children around; also because we have not yet finished our development, which was our original purpose for living. This answers the question raised in Chapter V. Death is just the end of *biological life*, not the end of *development*.

In the First Edition, I stated: "Our Parent is fully developed; we are not. It would take many lifetimes to achieve a level of development worthy of comparison with that of Our Parent." Now I believe that Our Parent is continuing to develop as well. If man has free will and if some part of the universe is chaotic, Our Parent will experience things never encountered before—imagined, maybe, but never encountered. That implies an opportunity to learn, and therefore develop. Interestingly, the need for continuing development is why reincarnation is one of the most important tenets of the great Eastern religions. Man will continue living his life over and over until he gets it right. Rarely does an individual achieve such a level in only one lifetime.

But it should be so much easier to develop freed from the constraints of our earthly environment and directly in the presence of Our Parent. Whereas before, we had to infer Our Parent, there we will see Our Parent in all His/Her wonderfulness. Our Parent will no longer have to hold back from making His/Her presence blatantly obvious to avoid contaminating our free will or violating the laws of probability.

On the other hand, something tells me that we

will not have everything laid out for us in one fell swoop. As humans, our greatest satisfaction comes when we surmount great obstacles to obtain something. We are happier with what we have earned than with what someone has handed to us.

Thus, I reason that Our Parent will not suddenly transform us from humans into some other form such that nothing of our former humanness remains. I think Our Parent will preserve and augment the good parts of our humanness, enhancing our ability to develop. We will still feel a challenge. We will still take pride in personal growth.

That kind of heaven sounds appealing to me. The angel-ly, harp-py kind does not.

Along the same line, I would hope that Our Parent would preserve something of our human heritage. As earthly parents, we preserve and point with pride and affection at the artifacts that commemorate the accomplishments of our children. My mother, to her dying day (at age 93), still kept on either side of her kitchen window a set of dopey ceramics that I had painted as a ten year old. They were sloppily and unevenly done and they clashed horribly with the decor of all of the kitchens we had throughout my Dad's long military career, but she didn't care. Up they went and there they stayed. From bronzed baby shoes, to graduation pictures, to bowling trophies, to whole rooms left "just as they were" at the death of a loved one, these things are important to us and are symbols of our love for one another.

VIII: Afterlife: Reward & Punishment

Eventually our Earth will pass away. In eight billion years, give or take a billion or so, our sun will have used up all its hydrogen fuel and will no longer be able to sustain life. Even if we have developed the technology to move away from the Earth in time and find another planet, eventually the same thing will happen to that sun and planet also. Eight billion years is a blink in eternity.

What then will happen to the great works of man: the beauty of Michelangelo's Sistine Chapel; the symphonies of Brahms; the Constitution of the United States; Japanese gardens; novels like *The Great Gatsby*; the pyramids and statues of Egypt; movies like *Casablanca*, and *To Kill a Mockingbird*; Fred Astaire and Ginger Rogers dancing to Cole Porter's *Night and Day*; and the untold treasures of tomorrow? I have to believe that Our Parent will find a place for these somehow in the afterlife.

Why? Because, these have contributed so much to human development. They are our starting point and they represent our progress at various stages of our development. They are more than the dopey ceramics and bowling trophies of our youth. I cannot believe that Our Parent will throw them away.

Let's discuss for a moment the idea of the promise of an afterlife as a motivator or deterrent. Although the heaven I have described is appealing to me, it is not really a "grabber." It certainly lacks the instant appeal and vividly explicit images of Mohammed's heaven. So I would not think, "Boy, I can hardly wait to get there," and step cheerfully in front of a bus to get there faster.

To be effective, motivators and deterrents must be fairly immediate. In the Old Testament, sin was apt to be punished immediately and visibly, by plague, loss of lands, war, and/or death. It was not good to get Jehovah mad at you. On the other hand, telling high school kids of thirteen or so that if they abstain from smoking and drinking you will buy them a car on their twenty-first birthday, may not deter them too much when they are out celebrating after a football victory. And telling a teen-ager to stay out of the sun because she'll have wrinkled skin when she is sixty is not likely to send her screaming from the beach wrapped in a towel from head to foot. She will more likely say something like, "Get real," then adjust her straps for more even tanning.

Besides, I do not believe that Our Parent wants us to come to Him/Her solely out of the promise of a reward or the threat of a punishment. As earthly parents, we are careful not to promise or threaten too much. We want our children to do good things out of love and a sense of responsibility, not because they will get something positive or negative out of it.

Also, just as Our Parent has not been blatantly obvious as to His/Her presence and power, thus pretty much forcing us to believe, Our Parent has not been blatantly obvious about heaven or hell. If Our Parent called a world meeting, opened the skies and said "Here's heaven," then opened the Earth and said "Here's hell," I am sure we would all tread more carefully, at least for a while. Since Our Parent has not seen fit to do this (at least as far as I know), He/She did not mean the afterlife primarily as a motivator or deterrent, but something else. How about punishment? In our earthly justice system, we often debate whether the objective of prison is retribution or rehabilitation. We might ask the same of hell.

I have read of parents who were so discouraged by the behavior of a son or daughter, usually in adolescence or beyond, that they disowned them and vowed never to see them again. In some of those absolutely heart-rending cases, the parents had been subjected to cruel abuse, and no one could blame them for feeling that way. But even then, if the parents thought that there was a way for their offspring to be saved, it is very hard for them to completely write off their own flesh and blood.

I believe that Our Parent must feel the same way, and that eternal punishment is not the fate of even the most villainous people that ever lived. Eventually even the worst may be forgiven.

But how do the lost earn forgiveness? Will they simply be returned to the fold after they have been roasted long enough?

That does not seem likely. What seems more likely to me is that Our Parent will give the lost souls an opportunity to continue to use their free will to seek forgiveness. Our Parent would require true repentance, not the sort of repentance that comes from being caught or being tortured. He/She does not want "crocodile" tears. How Our Parent would accomplish this is not clear to me, but I believe this view is consistent with the view of God as Our Parent.

And who are the lost souls? As a child, one does not have the opportunity to commit any big sins; the first real opportunity comes in adolescence (i.e., high school). I attended a Catholic high school, and I remember the following discussion we had in religion class with one of the priests. "You mean, Father, that we could live like a saint our whole lives, then commit a mortal sin at the last minute, and if we didn't get to Confession before we died we would go straight to hell?" "Or we could sin all over the place our whole lives and if there was a priest walking past as we were dying, we could make a quick Confession and go straight to heaven?"

The answer to our hypothetical was "Yes" in both cases. But, the priest said, that was unlikely to happen. If you had been leading a good life, chances were that you would not commit a mortal sin at the last minute, and vice-versa. Faced with a growing array of really neat and hard-to-resist temptations, we were pretty uncomfortable with the answer. On several occasions after I had succumbed, I went rushing around to find a priest and was a nervous wreck until I had found one to give me absolution.

I believe now that the real answer is that Our Parent would (as we would as parents) come out on the side of mercy, not justice. A last-minute save is as good as a lifetime of virtue. I believe that the priest was right, however: it is a poor bet to think that you will be lucky enough to obtain a just-in-time redemption at the end of a lifetime of vice. And if we stumble a bit near the end of an otherwise highly-developed life it makes sense to think that Our Parent will not abandon us at that late date.

I have asserted earlier that the purpose of life is to develop, but I have been a little short on how to do it. Actually, I believe that one of the best sources for helping us develop is the Bible. What??? After my seeming to utterly dismiss it? Well I believed I needed to put the Bible in context first. Now I'll suggest how to read it.

IX: How to Read the Bible

In writing this book, I have avoided the use of "authoritative sources," such as the Bible. I wanted to be able to say: "This and such are so because the Bible tells me so," but I felt I could not. In fact, that frustration led to my writing this book in the first place.

The problem is that so much of the Bible, both Old and New Testaments, seems confusing and contradictory to me. I had three choices: I could *accept* everything; I could *reject* everything; or I could *cherry-pick*, taking only the ideas from the Bible that appealed to me.

I found that I could not accept everything. If the Bible were inspired by God, such that it should be considered literal truth, why was it so inconsistent? I was unwilling to accept the inconsistencies as mysteries beyond human understanding. Thus I could not accept the Bible uncritically and use it as an authoritative source. God may have inspired the Bible, but it was edited by humans, not God.

Take the New Testament. The works of the Gospel authors are each taken to be written by one man; the discrepancies that exist are between one Gospel and another, not internally within the same Gospel. (I have read some claims that there was some tampering with the Gospels after they were written, however.) But the Old Testament seems to be different. As told by Richard Elliott Friedman, in *Who Wrote the Bible* (1987), for seventeen centuries after Christ it was assumed that each of the books of the Old Testament was written by a single author. In 1711, however, a German minister, Henning Bernard Witter, noticed some peculiarities. The same peculiarities were noted, apparently independently, by two other investigators: the first, Jean Astruca, a French medical doctor and court physician to Louis XV, in 1753; the second, Johann Gottfried Eichhorn, a German biblical scholar, in 1780.

The peculiarities first noted were two: first, there were doublets, two versions of events in the same story; second, quite often one of the versions would refer to God by one name, "God," the other version would refer to God by another name, "Yahweh."

Genesis is a good example. The first chapter of *Genesis* gives the sequence of creation as: 1) plants; 2) animals; and 3) man and woman together. The second chapter of *Genesis* tells the whole story over again, but this time the sequence of creation is: 1) man; 2) plants; 3) animals; and 4) woman. Read it yourself; it is quite fascinating.

By noting other consistent differences in style, language, and interests (one set of interests seemed to be priests, laws about priests, rituals, dates, measurements, sacrifice, etc.), later investigators have concluded that there are four different sources scattered about the first five books of the Bible, the Torah of Moses. The four different versions were cut up and combined into one long, continuous account.

Also, some of the stories in the Old Testament are downright scary: the *Book of Job*, for one. At one level, the story goes: Job is a man who is "perfect and upright;" Satan suggests to God that is because he is healthy and rich—take it away and Job will curse God; God afflicts Job with all sorts of calamities; Job bemoans his new state, but stays loyal to God; God then gave Job "twice as much as he had before." At that level, the lessons are fairly clear: have faith in God and you will be rewarded.

But on another level, are we humans simply pawns to be manipulated by God and Satan on some whimsical chessboard? I cannot believe that the story is literally true. The *Book of Job* is stirring, it is useful, and it is eerily beautiful, but it is not literal truth. It is most likely an allegory, a parable, rich in content and giving us enough to think about for the rest of our days.

Now take the New Testament again. In the New Testament, one aspect of human editing was the decision as to which of the candidate Gospels should be admitted into the Canon. There were many Gospels, now called the *Apocrypha*, which did not make the cut. Is it because they were not true, or because they did not fit into the mold of second-century orthodoxy? Luke himself, writing in the late first century, makes reference to other writings in the introduction to the Gospel ascribed to him: "Forasmuch as many have taken in hand to set forth in order a declaration of those things which are most surely believed by us ..."

A visiting theologian, in an interview with a reporter for our local newspaper, suggested that four gospels were chosen out of the many to preserve the symmetry with the "four corners of the earth." In Hugh J. Schonfield's *Original New Testament* (1985), these were: *Mark*, the West; *Matthew*, the South; *Luke*, the North; and *John,* the East. Schonfield also adds another likely reason: Already by the second century there were a variety of offshoots of Christianity promulgated by different teachers, such as Marcion and Cerinthus, and the Gnostics. Some were responsible for new Gospels. If the Four had not been made 'official' the Christian Church might well have disintegrated.

Having read some of these other Gospels, I can see why they might have been left out. Some are way more paradoxical than even the most difficult parables in the *Gospel of Mark*. The *Gospel According to Thomas*, discovered with other Coptic-Gnostic texts at Nag Hammadi in 1945, is a collection of the sayings of Jesus. Many of these sayings are obscure and puzzling enough to make the most ardent Zen Buddhist vibrate with pleasure. Other texts show Christ as uncomfortably human, preferring to nuzzle his girlfriend, Mary Magdalene, than to engage in spiritual discourse with his envious and grumbling disciples (the *Gospel of Phillip*).

All this—the inconsistency, the discrepancies, the political ramifications of choice, the differing versions within the same story, the obvious allegorical nature of some of the stories—left me unwilling to accept the Bible as the inspired, literal word of Our Parent. This left two choices: reject or cherry pick.

I was reluctant to reject the Bible because, despite the discrepancies, so much of it rang true in the concept of God as Our Parent. But with my feeble brain I was not sure I could always tell the difference between fact and allegory.

I was also reluctant emotionally because of the people whom I love who have such faith in it. What sums up this notion best for me is a continuation of the conversation I described earlier between Jurgen and God. Jurgen was speaking of belief in God, but he might just as well have been speaking of the Bible upon which the belief in God is based.

> God of my grandmother, I cannot quite believe in You; but remembering the sum of love and faith that has been given You, I tremble. I think of the dear people whose living was confident and glad because of their faith in You: I think of them, and in my heart contends a blind contrition, and a yearning, and an enviousness…I, Jurgen, see You only through a mist of tears. For You were loved by those whom I loved greatly a long time ago: and when I look at You it is Your worshipers and the dear believers of old that I remember.

Gulp! I remember my invalid grandmother inviting the priest (a wonderful guy with a thick Irish brogue) to come to the house to give her the sacraments, and then engaging him in great discussions. My mother would rather have faced a firing squad than to have missed Mass. Thus for me, as for Jurgen, letting go of the Bible as, well, *The Bible*, although intellectually defendable, is quite discomforting.

I was tempted to cherry pick, but that seemed dishonest. It is easy to prove a theory if you embrace all the data that support you and reject those that do not, although I would not be the first to do so.

In the end, I decided not to use the Bible at all in support of my theory of God as Our Parent. I have used other sources, as you will have noticed, but I have used them not as sources of literal truth but to give me ideas and to say things better than I could.

But that does not mean that we should reject the Bible totally; it only means that we should not expect to find objective truth there. Some have called the Bible, both Old and New Testaments, "Myth." I agree, to a point. But myth to me lacks any negative connotation whatever; myths have shown themselves vital to the development of the human race and myths can play an important role in our spiritual development as well. We just need to know how to use them properly.

All the stories we told our children helped them to look at the world in different ways. The classic myths from Homer's *Iliad* and *Odyssey*, to *Beowulf*, to the Arthurian legends, to the not-so-classic science fiction of today, have allowed us to examine our human condition freed from the conventions of day-to-day existence. The best of them are not influenced by dogma; in fact, stating some controversial ideas as myth has been one way of getting around an opposing dogma. In myths we can engage in non-linear, out-of-the-box thinking, explore "what ifs," and imagine ideal worlds.

We should not denigrate myths as being untrue. They have their own kind of truth.

One of the difficulties with the Bible is that it is a combination of myth and fact, and that it is very hard to tell the difference between them. It is hard to consider *Job* as anything but pure myth. Is the story of Noah and the flood a factual account, a myth, or a combination of the two? How much of the story of Christ is fact and how much is myth?

We could spend our time worrying about the differences, and many eminent scholars have done so, but this need not paralyze our thinking, even on that last item concerning the claimed divinity of Christ. What we need is a way to make the Bible useful to the development of a better relationship with Our Parent even if we cannot always tell the difference between "fact" and "myth."

Earlier, I talked about my aversion to cherry-picking. If I *were* going to cherry-pick, however, I would have done so in the New Testament, because Christ is such a remarkable figure. I would have ignored things that are the stuff of myth—like the virgin birth, the angels, the visitation by the Magi—

and concentrated on the person and message of Christ. Although we cannot be sure that Christ said or did any of the things he was reported to have said and done, the writers of the Gospels certainly portrayed an individual who had reached the highest level of development it is possible to reach.

But even the wonderful sketch of Christ's person and message seems to be colored by a certain amount of what might be second-century pessimism, and political and religious orthodoxy. One of the things that bothers me about the New Testament portrayal of Christ is what is *not* in there. Two things particularly: fun and sex.

"Jesus wept," is the shortest text in the New Testament. How nice it would have been for Christians if the Gospel writers had only thought to have included an equally short text, "Jesus laughed." We can infer that he laughed because of the company he is said to have kept: rough fishermen, publicans, the wealthy, the poor. He was invited to dinners and feasts where undoubtedly a lot of drinking was going on. Surely they would have stopped inviting him if he sat around like a spoil sport, frowning all the time. But including the words, "Jesus laughed," would have given more legitimacy to the idea that fun is O.K. I wish that Mark and company had included them. It would have made him seem more real.

What about sex? Christ must have had an imposing physical presence, and undoubtedly would have been attractive to women. It is easy to take that idea too far, however, and some have done so. Some of the portraits of Christ show him as somewhat namby pamby, with a soulful expression on his face, immaculately dressed and groomed: gown by Calvin Klein, hair by Monsieur Pierre, nails by Revlon. Nonsense. If Christ had been a carpenter, as some have claimed, he would probably have been bulging with muscles. If he was a trained Rabbi from the upper class, as others have suggested, well he still did a lot of walking. The distance from Capernaum, in Galilee, to Jerusalem is about seventy miles, and the route is not of Interstate quality. In any case, he was able to go into the presence of working fishermen, say "Follow me," and have them actually do it. Something about him was magnetic. Both men and women followed him, even, as the Gospel accounts report, to the foot of the cross.

The canonical Gospels do not report whether Christ was married or not, or whether he had sex or not. They are simply silent on the whole matter. Probably some of the apostles were married. Peter was, if the account is to be believed, because Christ is reported to have cured Peter's mother-in-law.

A non-canonical source, the *Gospel of Philip*, one of the Gnostic texts found in earthenware jars at Nag Hammadi, has the following intriguing lines concerning Christ's sexuality (taken from *The Other Bible* (1984) by Willis Barnstone):

> And the companion of the Savior is Mary Magdalene. But Christ loved her more than all the disciples and used to kiss her often on her mouth. The rest of the disciples were offended by it and

expressed disapproval. They said to him, 'Why do you love her more than all of us?' The Savior answered and said to them, 'Why do I not love you like her?'

An intriguing theory has arisen in the last few years concerning Christ and Mary Magdalene. (Actually, it is a theory that goes back to the beginning of the Church, but it was rediscovered only recently.) It appeared first in a book called *The Holy Blood and the Holy Grail*, by Michael Baigent, Richard Leigh, and Henry Lincoln (1982). The book and the theory made Margaret Starbird so mad and upset that she decided to do research to prove them wrong, but ended up embracing and enhancing the concept in a book of her own, called *The Woman with the Alabaster Jar* (1993).

The theory has also recently been popularized by the book, *The DaVinci Code*, which was written some seven years after the First Edition of this book came out, and it uses some of the same sources I used. I repeat it here in case you are one of the six people who has not read that fascinating book. The theory is this: Most people consider the Holy Grail as being the cup that Christ used at the Last Supper, a cup that was also used by Joseph of Arimathea to catch the last few drops of Christ's blood at the Crucifixion. Finding the Grail was the purpose of many a knightly quest back in the Middle Ages. Baigent, *et al.*, suggest that the real tenets of the Grail *legend* were really tenets of the Grail *heresy*: the Grail was not an earthen or metal cup; the Grail was Mary

Magdalene, the wife of Christ.

According to this theory, the blood of Christ was contained in the seed of Christ, which was deposited in her body during sexual intercourse. After the Crucifixion, as the wife of the "traitor" Jesus, the pregnant Mary Magdalene had to flee for her life, helped by Joseph of Arimathea, and ended up on the southern coast of France. The authors aver that the truth was ruthlessly suppressed by the Inquisition for centuries. I must say, both books are very meticulously researched and presented in a very scholarly and persuasive manner. I commend them for your reading.

Unfortunately, the canonical New Testament chose to portray the other side of Christ's life, leaving us to wonder about some of the things that would have made him seem more human to us. The Old Testament was more explicit about things like that, and I miss them in the New.

The Old Testament presents Solomon with his *Song of Songs*, a quite erotic celebration of the beauty of women: "Thy navel is like a round goblet, which wanteth not liquor: thy belly is a heap of wheat set about with lilies." (*Solomon 7*) With that line, no wonder he was able to attract "seven hundred wives, princesses, and three hundred concubines." (*I Kings 11*). The New Testament, on the other hand gives us Saint Paul with his "It is good for a man not to touch a woman...but if they cannot contain, let them marry: for it is better to marry than to burn." (*I Corinthians 7*). Obviously, somewhere between Solomon and St.

Paul somebody decided that sex was bad.

How can sex of itself be bad? It is certainly necessary for procreation. But beyond that, those of us lucky ones who have engaged in it know that sex is wonderful. Between two people who love each other, sex is one of the most powerful relationship-cementing activities we have. It is a way of our showing each other just how much we care. Of course, sex *abused* is bad, and we can abuse it like we can abuse anything else. Gastronomy abused becomes gluttony; relaxation abused becomes sloth and avoidance of responsibility; sex abused becomes obsession. Once again, it is a matter of balance.

But maybe the argument against it goes something like this: Christ was God, Christ never had sex, to emulate Christ one should not have sex. That was Paul's credo, and he lived it. Too bad.

Saint Paul made no bones about Christ being God. In *Romans*, Paul argued that Christ proved he was the "Son of God" (i.e., divine) by his resurrection from the dead. Then in *I Corinthians* he went so far as to say: "And if Christ be not risen, then is our preaching vain, and your faith is also vain." (I hope I am not distorting Paul's meaning by juxtaposing passages from two different letters.) I take Paul's statement to mean that the whole of Christianity is based upon the Resurrection. No Resurrection means no Divinity; no Divinity means no Christianity.

But you see, in contrast with the attitude of Saint Paul, to me, Christ is the more appealing if he is *not* divine, and has fun and sex with his fellow humans.

Otherwise, I tend to think, "Well of course he was able to do all that: he was God!"

But as non-God, he is absolutely remarkable. He is a hundred times the hero Beowulf ever was. Christianity does not depend on Christ's resurrection. Whether Christ was portrayed accurately or not, and whether he performed even one miracle or not, the real message of Christianity is that we—like Christ—can aspire to a close personal relationship with God, and that makes all the difference. Would Christ recognize Christianity as it is today with its rivalries and dogmatism and hierarchical structures? I'll let you answer that one for yourselves.

I hesitated to bring up the next subject lest my entire effort here be considered frivolous and myself considered "kooky."

But if you'll indulge me in a flight of fancy for a bit, a *future* argument that could cause us to reconsider our beliefs concerning the divinity of Christ will depend upon whether, as my English friend posited earlier, there is other intelligent life in the universe or not. Since my First Edition, scientists have begun to discover planets around many stars other than the sun. We do not yet know whether these planets are capable of supporting *any* life—let alone *intelligent* life—but the possibility is intriguing.

So let's first suppose there is. Presumably, considering the story of Adam and Eve as "true" for the moment—and that these other beings are not simply offshoots somehow of our own human race, with the same original parents—each of these other intelli-

IX: How to Read the Bible

gent species would have been tested in the same way as Adam and Eve. Presumably also, some of these species would have failed the test and some would have passed the test. The ones who have passed the test would then, if our traditions are correct, not be subject to disease and other human problems, including, some would say, death. This would make them a formidable species indeed, one that we would do well to invite to our planet.

But what of the ones that may have failed the test? Would these also have been redeemed, and by whom? Christ again, as a member of the other species? I cannot imagine a Parent who would send His/Her offspring, divine or not, to planet after planet to go through what Christ went through. Who else, then? Does God have other divine "Sons" or "Daughters" that would volunteer to do the redeeming?

If we are truly unique in the universe, then this whole line of thought goes away. If not, then this becomes an interesting consideration. At this point, nobody knows. I am convinced enough myself of the likelihood of other intelligent life, however, that this has served me as another (and certainly far down the scale) indication of the non-divinity of Christ. Why? Because I cannot imagine Christ going through all that more than once as a divine being, and the thought of other divine beings takes me too far from the concept of a diune God.

Well, to get back on the main track, I have said that: I cannot *accept* the Bible in its entirety as literal truth; I cannot *reject* the Bible, because undoubtedly some of it is literal truth; and I cannot *cherry pick* because I do not know how to tell the difference between literal truth and myth. Well, the latter is not quite true, because I *have* been doing some *cherry-picking* based on application of the Good Parent standard. But that has allowed me only to *reject* certain parts of the Bible which do not seem to meet the standard. I still cannot tell what parts I should *accept*. Where does that leave me/us?

In a good place, actually. Even with the difficulties I have noted with both Testaments, it would be difficult to imagine a richer, better source for discussion, reflection and inspiration. In the story of Abraham and Isaac (*Genesis* 22), for example, God asks Abraham to sacrifice his son as a test of his loyalty. Although torn between love for his son and love of God, Abraham prepares to perform the sacrifice, but an angel stays his hand, preventing him from carrying it out. Impressed and moved by the depth of Abraham's love, God makes Abraham the patriarch of the people of Israel. It is a wonderful story, illustrating the love and mercy of God and the reward for those who trust in the Lord. One could simply say that the mercy and love of God are great, and great is the reward for those who trust in Him, but the story conveys the idea much more vividly and memorably.

On the other hand, even so simple a story can have multiple meanings. Wilfred Owen, a poet of the First World War, took the story as a metaphor for life. Owen interpreted the story to mean that fathers should not be so quick to send their sons off to war to show loyalty to their country. His poem was later adapted by the composer Benjamin Britten for his *War Requiem*, one of the most hauntingly beautiful works ever written.

Perhaps a better way to think about the Bible is neither in terms of fact or myth (which terms are somewhat too pejorative anyway), but as "case study" material.

The Harvard Case Study Method was developed for the education of managers (and doctors, and lawyers) in recognition of the way in which people learn best: actively engaged in the learning process. Lectures are boring and uninvolving and the knowledge gained from them goes away quickly. People need context and reinforcement.

Case studies are considered by some to be part of a much larger category called Problem-based Learning. Don Margetson, of Griffith University, Queensland, contrasts it with Subject-based Learning in the following way in *The Challenge of Problem-Based Learning*, edited by David Boud and Grahame Feletti (1991). Subject-based Learning concentrates on content: to be an expert is to know a lot of content [my note: the *who*, *what*, *where*, and *when*]. Problem-based Learning concentrates on understanding [my note: the *how* and *why*]. If you hearken back to my discussion on learning for development, you will remember that the chief components of development were the understanding of *how* and *why*, so Margetson's notion fits nicely here.

Margetson goes on to list some characteristic advantages of Problem-based learning that I find quite pertinent (bracketed material [ ] is mine). Problem-based Learning:

> Encourages open-minded, reflective, critical and active learning. [Contrast that with passively listening to sermons.]

> Is morally defensible in that it pays due respect to both student and teacher [could be congregation and preacher, or any group having a discussion] as persons with knowledge, understanding, feelings and interests who come together in a shared educational process. [The minister, if there is one, acts as a facilitator, not an authority figure.]

> Reflects the nature of knowledge: that is, knowledge is complex and changes as a result of responses by communities of persons to problems they perceive in their worlds. [One could argue that the Bible is horribly out of touch with the problems of today—drugs, abortions, runaway technology, pollution—but it is amazing how current the Bible is in depicting the person-to-person interactions that will always be with us.]

Moreover, there is nothing like a story to give context and to help memory. One of my old bosses, a three-star Air Force general, said it rather nicely: "No one ever forgets what you tell them if you start out with the magic words: 'Once upon a time.'" Rather than present students with checklists of do's and don'ts for every situation, gleaned from the most successful practitioners of the management art, the Case Method (or Problem-based Learning scenarios, if you will) presents situations and stories and lets the budding managers discuss them. The situations and stories are taken from real life, but are often embellished or edited to focus upon the lessons the instructors are trying to get across. There are no "right" or "wrong" answers. "Success" comes from making the students more sensitive to potential problem and solution areas and more aware of the ramifications of their actions.

Having used the Case Method with students myself, I am intrigued that the lessons actually learned vary from group to group. In fact, I have never failed to have learned something new myself even though I have been through the same case numerous times. Thus it can be with the Bible as case study material.

The way to read the Bible, then, to be consistent with my thought process to date, is to read the various accounts, maxims, sayings, and depictions, holding them up to the standard of God as Our Parent. Many episodes of the Old Testament do not seem to meet that standard, but it is still useful to go through the exercise if only to say *how* and *why* the episode fails. Most episodes of the New Testament do meet the standard, probably because it is meant to depict God that way.

Now it is time to start putting all of this together.

X: Summing Up

What I have tried to do here is the opposite of what Saint Thomas Aquinas did. He started from a position of faith and tried to reconcile faith and reason. I started from a position of shattered faith and tried to reconcile reason and faith: to think myself into believing. I am not sure which was harder.

For me it meant following the path of the French philosopher, Rene Descartes, who realized that everything he knew or thought he knew was based upon some premise that may or may not have been true. He felt that he needed to strip away all of his assumptions and get down to something he knew for sure. As all of you know, the one thing he could be sure of was his own existence, which he proved to his own satisfaction by reasoning that if he did not exist, how could he think? "I think, therefore I am," is one of the most famous passages in all of philosophy.

I also felt the need to strip away all of my assumptions about God. Since most of my assumptions had come from the Catholic Church and the Bible—and since much of what I had been getting from those sources was confusing and contradictory to me—I felt that I could not continue to accept them uncritically.

When I started writing this treatise, I really did not know how it was going to turn out. I just knew that I could not continue as I was, going to church out of some combination of fear and habit, keeping my mind disengaged. In fact, I thought there was a real possibility that I might end up squarely back in the fold of the Catholic Church, strong in faith, doubting no more. I probably secretly hoped that would be the outcome. After all, that would entail the least change in my life and it would ease my feelings of guilt about abandoning the faith of my Catholic forebears.

But I have reasoned my way to a new faith. The core of that faith, the Cartesian irreducible basis, is that God exists and the best way to think of God is as Our Parent.

From this, all else follows. To wit:

Our Parent must have all the male and female characteristics that have been passed down to us. It is a mistake to think of Our Parent as Our Father alone.

Our Parent must be "good," or humans have no chance. We could not expect to get any help from a God that is evil or whimsical.

The purpose of life is not to serve Our Parent, but to develop fully as human beings.

Our Parent does not have a "will" for us, but hopes and aspirations.

Our Parent does not preordain anything and does not know how we will turn out.

Our Parent aids our development (through our

intuition channel) by helping us to help ourselves. Our Parent's aid will not be at the expense of violating anyone's free will or the laws of probability that run the universe.

Sin is anything that deliberately interferes with our development or the development of others. Even as gross a crime as genocide can be thought of in this way (although I would not want some smirking Nazi to describe it like that).

The afterlife is an opportunity for further development, unhampered by the earthly environment and enhanced by the more direct and closer relationship with Our Parent. Our Parent would never want to lose any of His/Her children, so there must be a chance to make up after death even for the worst of us.

The Bible and other such documents and traditions, although unreliable as literal, divinely-revealed truth, are still marvelous sources of case studies for our development, as long as we hold them to the standard of God as Our Parent: "Would Our Parent really do things that way?"

That is the track that takes me from reason to faith, and it has worked for me. But I can see that people from dysfunctional families might wonder what in the world I am talking about. For me, the concept of God as Our Parent comes naturally and easily. I was blessed with parents who embodied many of the ideals of the Good Parent, and they gave me a good reference for the way things ought to be. I knew that my parents loved me and were proud of me. I would have done almost anything to keep that love and trust. My dad, particularly, was my hero, although I loved my mother dearly as well. Probably my greatest motivation for walking the straight and narrow was because I wanted to be like my dad and because I did not want to do anything that would diminish me in his eyes. I did not fear my dad; I loved and respected him so much that losing the closeness of our relationship was unthinkable.

This is, I believe, the way Our Parent wants to be with us, and this is what the idea of "development" is all about. Our Parent does not want to be served, worshiped, feared, or enslaved by the need to do His/Her will. He/She does not want sheep. Our Parent wants us to develop, each in our own way as the individuals Our Parent made us.

I talked about this earlier as reasoning my way to a "new faith," but that is not true at all. I am suggesting that this is the way it should have been all along. For more than fifteen-hundred years, we humans accepted the Ptolemaic model in which the sun rotated around the earth. The model worked, but only by making a bunch of complicated corrections to account for some of the strange products of observation. Copernicus, by changing the model to one in which the earth rotated around the sun, made the need for all those complicated corrections go away. He employed Ockham's Razor: he simplified.

I believe that all I am doing here is simplifying, doing away with the need to make all of the complicated corrections necessary to reconcile the traditional beliefs about God with what our reason tells us must be so. And I believe that this is consistent with the notion of God as Our Parent. Why should Our Parent wrap Himself/Herself in a cloak of mystery and misunderstanding? We have done that, not Our Parent. We need to cut through all the mystery stuff and just get closer to someone who loves us dearly and wants us to get to know Him/Her better.

But, like Copernicus', my beliefs are at odds with the cherished beliefs of many people, and I am likely to be resented for my efforts. I do not wish to cause doubt in those who have none. As I said before, in some ways I envy their serenity. Each of us is responsible for our own development. Far be it from me to interfere in the development of others. My message is for those who do have doubts and who may have abandoned the search.

Perhaps some organized religion out there somewhere already embraces the tenets I have outlined here. I do not profess to have knowledge of all religions. But I deliberately did not want to go "religion shopping," wherein someone else would have done my thinking for me. I felt I had to sort it out myself. Now that I have done that, I will look around for other people and groups willing to share these ideas and feelings in not terribly structured ways. As I said before, there is synergy in mutual sharing: the whole is definitely greater than the sum of the parts. But I am wary of too much structure. Structure (to me, at least) eventually leads to dogma, hierarchy, and the shutting down of the intuitive

X: Summing Up

channels so necessary for unfettered communication.

It may be that even my own Catholic Church will eventually come around to espousing many of the principles presented here and I can rejoin it without feeling hypocritical. I doubt it though. The traditions are too strong.

What I am suggesting is a new paradigm for the relationship between man and God, and new paradigms do not usually take effect swiftly. Two quotes from Thomas Kuhn's book, *The Structure of Scientific Revolutions* (1962, 1970), tell the tale better than I could:

> Darwin, in a particularly perceptive passage at the end of his *Origin of Species*, wrote: 'Although I am fully convinced of the views given in this volume...I by no means expect to convince experienced naturalists whose minds are stocked with a multitude of facts all viewed, during a long course of years, from a point of view directly opposite to mine. ...[But] I look with confidence to the future—to young and rising naturalists, who will be able to view both sides of the question with impartiality.'

> And Max Planck, surveying his own career in his *Scientific Autobiography*, sadly remarked that 'a new scientific truth does not triumph by convincing its opponents and making them see the light, but rather because its opponents eventually die, and a new generation grows up that is familiar with it.'

On the other hand, despite their probable resistance to the new paradigm, I do not resent the Catholic Church in any way, nor do I regret my Catholic education. I have nothing but fond memories of the kind priests and nuns who did so much to shape me. They did their best from their own belief system and I cannot fault them for it. One of the major aims of the Jesuits was to teach us to think. Ironically, in many ways, this book is the result—unfortunate, perhaps, from their viewpoint, but wonderful from mine.

Whether or not anyone else accepts what I have written here, I will have accomplished my purpose, which was to help me develop a better relationship with God based upon love and understanding, not fear and superstition. The time I have spent on this book, many hours a day over many days, is the most time I have ever spent thinking about the spiritual side of my life. I have not been knocked off my horse with a blinding revelation, as Saint Paul is said to have been. My revelation has been quieter and more personal, and it is getting stronger all the time as I have put to practice some of these ideas. The most important things for me have been that I feel closer to God than I ever have, I now include God in more and more areas of my life, and I can see myself developing in ways I would never have considered before.

Do I claim to have all the answers? Of course not. Nor will I until I have completed my development in the afterlife (if that is even possible: it may be that only Our Parent will ever have all the answers). I do not even have all the questions. What I do have, however, are two things I have never had before: I have a new conception of God (Our Parent); and I have a standard against which I can begin to answer even the toughest questions ("How would Our Parent react to that?").

I feel that I now have a good starting point for my continued development and the tools and the will to carry it out. For me that is enough for now.

XI: Addendum: "What Then Must We Do?"

The quote above is from Luke, Chapter 3, Verse 10. John the Baptist had been admonishing the multitudes to "bring forth fruits in keeping with their repentance," and they wanted some specifics. He obliged at least some of them. Those with two tunics were exhorted to share with those who had none; tax gatherers and soldiers were given advice peculiar to their professions. Tolstoy wrote a whole book with the same title and was so affected by the implications of the question that he went into the poorest streets in Moscow and gave away all his money.

The reason I came up with this Addendum is a question that occurred to me after I had published the First Edition: what should I and society as a whole do with this new concept of God? I have described a God that is pretty much hands-off. He/She created us and left us as persons and as a society to develop largely on our own: willing to guide us through our intuition channel, but no physical miracles; no interference with our free will; no knowledge about what we will do with our free

XI: Addendum: What Then Must We Do?

will; and (since I dismissed the Bible as objective and absolute truth) no explicit instructions on how to proceed. What then must we do?

I presented the idea of *development* as the primary goal of life, even going so far as to describe heaven as an opportunity for accelerated and advanced development. As individuals, if we are all busily trying to grow and advance ourselves, we will have less chance of getting into mischief with ourselves, our surroundings and our fellow humans. The US Army's slogan, "Be all that you can be," is a wonderful slogan—as long as one understands that it describes a moving goal. One should be better tomorrow than one is today.

And what about society as a whole? As John Donne (1572-1631) writes:

> No man is an island entire of itself; every man is a piece of the continent, a part of the main; if a clod be washed away by the sea, Europe is the less, as well as if a promontory were, as well as any manner of thy friends or of thine own were; any man's death diminishes me, because I am involved in mankind. And therefore never send to know for whom the bell tolls; it tolls for thee.

It is not enough for individuals to develop; society needs to develop as well. Thomas Jefferson put it very well in the Declaration of Independence:

> We hold these truths to be self-evident, that all men are created equal, that they are endowed by their Creator with certain unalienable Rights,

that among these are Life, Liberty and the pursuit of Happiness. —That to secure these rights, Governments are instituted among Men, deriving their just powers from the consent of the governed.

The governors and the governed need to be involved in the development process or the justice and rights will be lost.

But how do individuals and societies develop? Development is a process of identifying opportunities for advancement (and those things that might be holding you back), of taking action to progress (or avoiding actions that would impede your progressing), of measuring your progress, then applying what you have learned to your next stage of development. Continuously. But development should be based upon sound moral principles, otherwise you are "growing as a cemetery grows," not really advancing. We are aware of general admonitions such as Robert Browning's, "Mans' reach should exceed his grasp, or what's a heaven for," (*Song from Pippa Passes*) but we need more.

Man's idea of morality has traditionally come from religion, and much of that has come from the Bible and other religious texts. But my "fresh look at God" downgraded the Bible into myth and called into question the authority of its moral message. In doing so, the Ten Commandments went from the realm of divine imperative to something much less.

Here's the dilemma: If moral principles cannot be simply lifted from the Bible and the Ten Commandments, where *can* we get them? Nietzsche and others have suggested that without God there is no morality. So where are we if (as I suggest) God is different than depicted in traditional sources: a God instead who is not hands on, but allowing us to develop pretty much on our own? Worse yet, what if there really is no God? Where do Jefferson's "just powers" come from then?

The answer for me is that we need to lay out a set of secular moral principles that might augment or even replace the religion-based ones. As author Robert Ruark suggested, the bloody, anti-white Mau Mau uprising (1952-60) in Kenya, Africa resulted from the Europeans taking away the black man's beliefs and institutions and not replacing them with "Something of Value." So far, I have attacked traditional sources but have not suggested good alternatives.

And time may be running out for this. About three years ago I became concerned that morality was no longer being taught in secular schools. Not that anything special had happened; the thought had finally broken through my threshold of alarm, that's all. My evidence was almost entirely anecdotal, but it was easy to see why this might have been happening. We have all watched as our increasingly diverse, politically-correct, church/state-separating nation has used the constitutional provision, "Congress shall make no law respecting an establishment of religion, or prohibiting the free exercise thereof," to turn all public places into God-free zones. So plaques containing the Ten Commandments are ripped down from courtroom walls and teachers tend to avoid the subject of morality entirely. The marks of the plaques are still on the wall, but nothing of value has replaced them.

So I began to think about a new set of morality-based principles—not obviously taken from Judeo-Christian theology—that *could* perhaps be taught in schools and placed on the walls of public buildings. (Although perhaps not placed on courtroom walls: I understand the argument that judicial decisions should be based upon the law only. One would hope that the laws themselves are based upon morality—although clearly some have not been—but that is another discussion for another day.)

Thus I have come up with a set of eleven moral principles—listed below in the form of "personal pledges." They are not in any particular order, because I could think of situations in which the order of importance might change. They lack both the *sturm und drang* and the implied threat resulting from non-compliance with the Commandments (the "BECAUSE I SAID SO:" signed, God). Also, the discussions about them in this book will be relatively brief because I think I would muck up the principles by over explaining them. The Ten Commandments are not explained in the Old Testament either. Think of the eleven pledges as a personal and societal moral/developmental checklist to guide what to do and what not to do. All are positive: there are no "shalt nots."

XI: Addendum: What Then Must We Do?

As with any list, what is NOT there may be more important than what IS there. I leave it to you, dear reader, to critique the list and to add and subtract as your (developed) conscience directs.

I PLEDGE TO

BE KIND TO MY NEIGHBOR
TAKE RESPONSIBILITY FOR MY ACTIONS OR INACTIONS
SUPPORT JUST CAUSES AND OPPOSE UNJUST ONES
HELP THOSE WHO CANNOT HELP THEMSELVES
REACH MY FULLEST POTENTIAL
PROTECT AND IMPROVE THE ENVIRONMENT
SUBMIT TO LAWFUL AUTHORITY
MAINTAIN A HIGH STANDARD OF PERSONAL MORALITY
BE TRUE TO MY WORD
PARTICIPATE IN THE POLITICAL PROCESS
MAINTAIN A REVERENCE FOR LIFE

As you can easily see, each of these is pregnant with opportunities for vastly different interpretation. Well, so are the Ten Commandments; so are the short articles of the Constitution. But in my judgment, that makes them more powerful.

Will there ever be universal, precise agreement about concepts like "kindness," or "neighbor," for example?" Of course not. Christ explained who a neighbor was with his beautiful story of the *Good Samaritan*. Someone today might conclude that it is more kind to force a person off welfare rather than continue to feed (and share a cloak with) him. Poet Steven Crane (1905) wrote "Do not weep, maiden, war is kind." The conventional interpretation of this is that Crane was being ironic. To the "Mother whose heart hung humble as a button on the bright splendid shroud of your son," war was anything but kind. My own additional interpretation is that Crane viewed death in war as truly kind in the sense that it was a release both from war itself and from the misplaced glory sought by "little souls that thirst to fight." It doesn't bother me that people will read different things into the pledges. The important thing is the discussion.

How about questions of degree? How much should we "support just causes and oppose unjust ones?" To the death? How lawful should "lawful authority" be before we agree to submit to it? It's a complex world; there are no easy answers or interpretations.

What happened in this construct to supposedly absolute commandments such as, "Thou Shalt Not Kill?" Well, as at least mentioned earlier, killing is sometimes justified—to prevent a felony, for example. The concept of justified or unjustified killing can be debated under several of the principles above. It even gives a framework for discussion of modern highly-charged conundrums about euthanasia, abortion, cloning and the like.

My original thought was that these principles could be placed on the wall of a classroom and discussed with children. I still believe that would be of great benefit to them and to society. No doctrinal tenets need be invoked. The teacher could take a

Socratic stance, getting the children to come to their own (guided) conclusions about the benefits and/or consequences of following or failing to follow the principles. On the other hand, a religiously-oriented school might have some definite ideas about these principles and press their viewpoints vigorously.

To review, the point of this chapter is that, having called into question traditional sources of moral thought and guidance such as the Bible, I felt I had to come up with "something of value" to replace them. You will be the judge of how well I have succeeded. You may well say several smack of New-Age thinking, tree-hugging environmentalism, Kumbaya hand-holding feelgoodism, or other indications of our current penchant for moral feebleness; your privilege. But I have discussed these with several friends (who are friends enough to let me know if I am totally wacko) and I believe they can indeed make a positive contribution in our present political and spiritual climate. At least, I hope they'll do until something better comes along.

I wish you well in your developmental journey.

Bibliography

Armstrong, Karen, *A History of God* (New York: Ballantine Books, 1993).

Asimov, Isaac, *Understanding Physics* (Dorset Press, 1966).

Barnstone, Willis, *The Other Bible* (San Francisco: Harper, 1984).

Baigent, Michael, Richard Leigh, and Henry Lincoln, *The Holy Blood and the Holy Grail* (London: Jonathan Cape, Ltd., 1982) reprinted as *Holy Blood, Holy Grail*, (New York: Dell Publishing Company, 1983).

Boud, David, and Grahame Feletti, Eds., *The Challenge of Problem Based Learning* (New York: St. Martin's Press, 1991).

Cabell, James Branch, *Jurgen* (New York: Grosset and Dunlap, 1919).

Carroll, James, *An American Requiem* (Boston:

Houghton Mifflin Co., 1996).

Durant, Will, *Caesar and Christ* (New York: Simon and Schuster, 1944).

Durant, Will, Our *Oriental Heritage* (New York: Simon and Schuster, 1954).

Friedman, Richard Elliott, *Who Wrote the Bible?* (New York: Summit Books, 1987).

Freud, Sigmund, *Civilization and its Discontents* (New York: W.W. Norton & Co., written in 1930; translated and edited by James Strachey, 1961).

Gleik, James, *Chaos: Making a New Science* (New York: Penguin Books, 1987).

Gray, John, *Men are from Mars, Women are from Venus* (New York: Harper Collins, 1992).

Harmon, Michael M., and Richard T. Mayer, *Organization Theory for Public Administration* (Boston: Little Brown and Co., 1986).

Kuhn, Thomas S., *The Structure of Scientific Revolutions*, 2nd Ed. (Chicago: The University of Chicago Press, 1970).

Mack, Burton L., *The Lost Gospel* (San Francisco: Harper, 1993).

Mack, Burton L., *Who Wrote the New Testament?* (San Francisco: Harper, 1995).

Mitroff, Ian, *Stakeholders of the Organizational Mind* (San Francisco: Jossey-Bass Publishers, 1983).

Pirsig, Robert M., *Zen and the Art of Motorcycle Maintenance* (New York: William Morrow and Co., Inc., 1974).

Schonfield, Hugh J., *The Original New Testament* (San Francisco: Harper and Row, 1985).

Wilson, A.N., *Jesus: A Life* (New York: Fawcett Columbine, 1992).

About the Author

Charles P. Cabell Jr. is a 1958 graduate of the United States Military Academy at West Point. He holds a Masters Degree (Astronautics) from the Air Force Institute of Technology and a Masters Degree (Systems Management) and Doctoral Degree (Public Administration) from the University of Southern California. He retired from the Air Force as a Brigadier General after a thirty-year career (which included a combat flying tour in Vietnam), and spent nine years as a consultant to industry and the government in the areas of System Engineering, Risk Management, and Project Management.

Fully retired now, he lives with his wife in Colorado Springs. He has two grown children—a daughter and a son—and five grandsons. He now devotes much of his life to writing and publishing (www.impavidepublications.com).

He is also quite active in music. He studies classical piano privately and he is a former member of the Colorado Springs Chorale and the Colorado Springs Opera Chorus and he has written folk songs and choral pieces. In addition, he has over 1500 classical music phonograph records. In 1999, he co-founded Amateur Pianists International, an organization that presents the annual *Celebration of the Amateur Pianist*, which includes the *Rocky Mountain Amateur Piano Competition* and other musical activities (www.apiano.org).

www.ingramcontent.com/pod-product-compliance
Lightning Source LLC
LaVergne TN
LVHW041628070426
835507LV00008B/509